Cubesat Operations

How to fly Cubesats

© 2017, 2021

Patrick H. Stakem

2nd in the Cubesat Series

Table of Contents

Goals for the Book

This book can be used as a reference text for an undergraduate or graduate course, or for an individual wishing to learn more about the technology. It is the author's intent that the reader will:

- Understand the processing of data from the Cubesat, and the command data to the Cubesat.
- Understand the architecture of the Cubesat Control Center, and how it is evolving.
- Understand the functions that the Control Center implements.
- Understand the implementation of maintenance of the control center.
- Understand the Control Center's role in normal and contingency operations.
- Understand the critical importance of control center and link security.
- Understand the role of the Control Center in the Integration and Test Phase, and for training.
- Understand the roles of the operations support team, and how the members interact.
- Understand how certain routine tasks can be automated.
- Be able to serve as a member of a Cubesat Operations Team.
- Be able to pass these skills along to others.

Introduction

This book covers the topic of satellite control centers for Cubesats. We'll take a look at some of the historical development of satellite control centers. Mention a spacecraft control center, and every one remembers the one from the movie Apollo-13. A cubesat control center can be implemented on a laptop. We'll look at the evolution of satellite control centers to understand how we got to where we are, and we'll look at evolving technology to see where we can go.

As technology advances, we have a better technology basis for control centers, as well as cheaper yet more capable hardware, and better and more available software. With the proliferation of inexpensive Cubesat projects, colleges and universities, high school, and even individuals are getting their Cubesats launched. They all need control centers. For lower cost missions, these can be shared facilities. Communicating with and operating a spacecraft in orbit or on another planet is challenging, but is an extension of operating any remote system. We have communications and bandwidth issues, speed-of-light communication limitations, and complexity. Remote debugging is a always a challenge.

The satellite control center is part of what is termed the Ground Segment, which also includes the communication uplink and downlink. The control center generates uplink data (commands) to the spacecraft, and receives, processes, and archives downlink (telemetry) data. The spacecraft is usually referred to as the space segment. The spacecraft usually consists of a "bus", the engineering section, and the payload, either a science instrument package or a communications package. Satellite buses can be "off-the-shelf," leading to economies of scale. This is the Cubesat way.

I am not going to tell you how to implement a satellite control center, but rather what its functions are. They are many commercial products that can be used, and a few open source options. Don't re-invent the wheel. NASA has been updating its control center and mission operations to accommodate Cubesats, and a pointer to that work is included. This book also addresses the topic of Control Center as a service (in the Cloud), and flying the control center, for constellations.

This book is a companion to the Cubesat Engineering book by the author.

This book was compiled from ITAR-compliant sources.

Author

Mr. Patrick H. Stakem has been fascinated by the space program since the Vanguard launches in 1957. He received a Bachelors degree in Electrical Engineering from Carnegie-Mellon University, and Masters Degrees in Physics and Computer Science from the Johns Hopkins University. At Carnegie, he worked with a group of undergraduate students to re-assemble and operate a surplus Athena missile guidance computer. It was brought up to operational status, and modified for general purpose use.

He began his career in Aerospace with Fairchild Industries on the ATS-6 (Applications Technology Satellite-6), program, a communication satellite that developed much of the technology for the TDRSS (Tracking and Data Relay Satellite System). He followed the ATS-6 Program through its operational phase, and worked on other projects at NASA's Goddard Space Flight Center including the Hubble Space Telescope, the International Ultraviolet Explorer (IUE), the Solar Maximum Mission (SMM), some of the Landsat missions, and others. He was posted to NASA's Jet Propulsion Laboratory for MARS-Jupiter-Saturn (MJS-77), which later became the *Voyager* mission, and is still operating and returning data from outside the solar system at this writing.

Mr. Stakem is affiliated with the Whiting School of Engineering of the Johns Hopkins University, and Capitol Technology University.

Control Center – what it is, what it does

A satellite control center has a wide variety of tasks. It provides services to the mission 24x7x365. These services include the reception, archiving, limit-checking, and conversion of the received telemetry data. Today, received telemetry is archived in raw form, and saved in engineering units in a database. Use of a standard commercial database simplifies operations and controls costs. The Control Center disseminates selected data to users, either located in a control room, or via the web. The Control Center is usually built around a STOL, or scripting language, for automation of operations where possible. The software does limit checking of incoming data, and issues alerts if limits are exceeded. The control center also is responsible for commanding the spacecraft. This is all true for a Cubesat Mission, but is in some ways simpler. The same functions have to be addressed. This book covers the care and feeding of a deployed cubesat.

Early in the Mission definition phase, various Operations Concepts (Ops Concepts) are defined, and these lead to requirements. The Ops Concepts drive the architecture of the Control Center. There must be sufficient flexibility for the Ops Concepts to evolve, as the mission progresses.

The Control Center provides work space, data systems for telemetry, command capability, and coordination of activities between subsystems. The Control Center is responsible for spacecraft planning and scheduling. It is usually operating 24 x 7. The Control Center becomes a busy place during launch and spacecraft anomaly or failure situations. It is the workplace for the flight operations team. Generally, the Control Center has a front room, and a back room. The front room is responsible for all real time activities, and commanding. The back room is for off-line analysis. Different personnel may inhabit the back room at different times and mission mission phases. In the early days of spacecraft, the control center function was done from the launch site, or a tracking station. As spacecraft computers become more powerful, and the communications improve, some of the functions of the control center can be done onboard. In addition, the control center architecture has evolved from mainframe computers, to the client-server architecture, to pc's, and then to distributed models, based on the cloud. It is important, though, to still have a defined control center "space" where the operations team can congregate.

Here are some of the tasks that need to be done to support a space mission. Not all are applicable to all missions. The Control Center can be large and complex, such as the entire building for the

Hubble Space Telescope, or simple, like a laptop-based control center for a Cubesat. Here are some of the tasks done in the Control Center.

- Planning and Scheduling
- Commanding
- Onboard engineering support (housekeeping)
- Data archiving
- Performance monitoring, fault detection, and diagnostics
- Calibration

We'll discuss how and where these functions are implemented later. Some of these functions can be automated, and some can be accomplished onboard. With a Cubesat mission, it is entirely possible to host the control center functionality on a single laptop.

Functional areas of the Control Center include Flight/Mission Control (Systems level) Guidance, Navigation, and Attitude Control, Thermal monitoring, Electrical Power, Onboard Computer and Data System, Communications and RF, and Payload Operations. Each of these generally maps to a seat in the Control Center, with a Team lead, typically a Systems Engineer, in charge.

The Planning and Scheduling function is off-line, ahead of the time it will be needed. It results in a detailed, optimized schedule of operations, for a 24-hour period or longer. It may involve complex predictive modeling of the spacecraft and its environment. Once the time-line is verified, it will be mapped into commands sent to the spacecraft for execution. There are also contingencies for special conditions and anomalies. These are all done ahead of when they are needed.

Some items that might have to be factored into the time-line include entrance and exit from the South Atlantic Anomaly (SAA) trapped radiation zone, which might require turning off certain sensitive equipment. There is also the issue of Earth occultation (when the spacecraft is on the opposite side of the Earth from the Sun, and thus has no solar power), and possibly a lunar eclipse, which will also block the Sun.

If we are relying on sensing the Earth's rim to keep pointing to a desired terrestrial target, we must also know when the Sun will blind the horizon sensor. It is also possible that the moon will be partially obscured by the Earth from the spacecraft's point of view, and a horizon sensor would see that as a "bigger" Earth. We need to know when the spacecraft is in line-of-sight of a ground station.

And then, there's orbital decay and debris to worry about. Due to the very small but finite atmosphere, there is orbital drag. A strong Solar Wind or Solar storm can also affect the orbit. Orbital debris is an increasing problem. Each mission is now required to have an end-of-life plan, usually involving reentry. There are literally hundreds of thousands of insert orbital objects tracked, from upper stage boosters, to zombie-sats, to bolts. At the orbital speeds involved, even a grain of dust can carry significant energy to be a lethal projectile. These data are available from a NORAD website. Another set of data that is needed in scheduling is the Ephemeris of the satellite, its position and path. Both of these items will be discussed later in the book.

Engineering support, or housekeeping activities, are accomplished according to schedule, or in response to conditions. An example is momentum unloading. To keep properly oriented, the spacecraft may use momentum wheels. These are spun at high speed to move the much more massive spacecraft in the opposite rotation, slowly. The problem is, there are biases in the gravity field that cause the momentum wheels to become saturated at some point, days, usually. How can we get rid of this momentum, there's nothing to push against? Actually, there is. We can push against the Earth's magnetic field. That requires a map of the field, from the spacecraft's point of view. Momentum wheel unloading can be adjusted accordingly.

Another commodity that has to be tracked is the amount of onboard storage for data. This might fill up, and need to be "dumped" to the ground when a communication channel is available. The spacecraft will need to point its solar arrays for getting the maximum power, its communication antenna to get the best signal, and perhaps movable parts of the science payload, to keep the target in view.

Onboard status monitoring is common today, but should still be backed up with ground-based monitoring and trending. It is usual to have spare components (4 momentum wheels when we only need three; redundant radios, etc). Spares management and planning for "Plan B"is critical when configuration changes are needed due to degradations and failures. Part of this can be derived from a good Failure Modes and Effects Analysis (FMEA) done during the design and testing process, and kept updated throughout the program.

Historical Examples

How do we talk and listen to satellites, send them commands, and receive their data? How did satellite control centers evolve? This is a data question. The radio portion of the uplink (to the satellite) and downlink (from the satellite) is off-the shelf. Satellites can now be considered as nodes on a network, which means we have fewer details to worry about. Initially, computers were big, unique, heavy mainframes with a dedicated priesthood of programmers and system engineers to keep them running. They were enshrined in specially air conditioned rooms with raised floors and access control. They ran one job at a time, taking punched cards as input, and producing reams of wide green-striped paper output. Data were collected on reels of magnetic tape, or large trays of punched cards. Access to these very expensive resources was necessarily limited.

Then, a better idea evolved. Most of the time, the "big iron" was not computing, it was waiting. So, if we could devise a way to profitably use the idle time, we would increase the efficiency of the facility. This lead to the concept of time-sharing. There was a control program whose job it was to juggle the resources so that a useful program was always running. This came along about the time that remote terminals were hooked to the mainframe, to allow access from multiple, different locations. In a sense, the computer facility was virtualized; each user saw his or her very own machine (for limited periods of time, anyway). If the overhead of switching among users was not too great, the scheme worked well.

This evolved into a "client-server" socket-type architecture, in which the mini-computer based remote clients had some compute and storage capability of their own, but still relied on the server.

In the background, something else amazing was happening. Mainframes were built from relays and vacuum tubes, magnetic core memory, and massive rotating magnetic drums for storage. Eventually, semiconductor devices began to take over. Semiconductor technology scales nicely. In fact, Gordon Moore of Intel formulated his famous law from observations that the complexity of the devices doubled every 18 months. This is an exponential growth curve. If we have 1 unit of memory in a package for a certain cost, in 18 months we will have 2 units of memory in the same package for the same price. In 18 more months, 4 units, and so on.

It doesn't take long for this to really add up. And, the technology feeds on itself. The computers used to design and manufacture chips keep getting more and more capable.

Now, our phones have orders-of-magnitude more compute and storage capability than mainframes did. My tablet has more capability than my entire University had when I was an undergraduate. Such exponential growth laws can't be sustained forever, but, so far, so good.

Communications, drawing on the same technology, has vastly

improved as well. NASA's data transmission system in the early days used their own and leased landlines, with ships and aircraft to fill in the gaps over the ocean. Now, satellite data is relayed between spacecraft, and a series of geostationary Tracking and Data Relay Satellites allow for almost complete coverage. Data that used to travel over dedicated lines now moves on the Internet infrastructure, which includes ground and under-sea fiber optic cable, and communications satellites as well. Coverage is provided to the Polar regions by communications satellites in Polar orbit. Yes, Antarctica has good Internet coverage.

Rapid changes in technology that effect how we do things, or enable us to do new things, are called paradigm shifts. Sometimes these are gradual, and sometimes abrupt. Get used to it. We'll examine some of the historical and evolutionary satellite control centers. The Architecture evolved into a workable system, and we use this today, albeit implemented in different technologies. Today, do you want to get your satellite data on your smart watch? – no problem. Cubesats represent paradigm shifts in how we do space missions.

Unmanned missions, near-Earth

NASA's unmanned near-earth missions are the responsibility of the Goddard Space Flight Center in Greenbelt, Maryland. Initially, control centers were as different and unique as the early spacecraft themselves. As more satellite series came along (TDRSS, NOAA weather satellites) there was a corresponding similarity in control centers.

These spacecraft are built on same standardized bus architecture, and may have the same payload. An early example of this was GSFC's MultiMission Modular Spacecraft (MMS), which could support a wide variety of missions, and was compatible with the shuttle for launch, retrieval, and servicing. The Hubble Space Telescope is build on the MMS bus.

Building 14 was the operational nerve center for NASA Goddard

Missions. An early control room for the orbiting Astronomical Observatory (OAO) was located in the basement of Building 14.

During launch operations, the mission control room monitors the satellite(s), referred to as the "payload." The launch control center has control of the mission at this time, until the payload separates from the launch vehicle. This is usually within 10-15 minutes after launch, and the control center takes over.

POCC

The Payload Operations Control Center (POCC) was a concept developed at GSFC to leverage the similarity of spacecraft using the MMS. Rather than design each control center from scratch, a baseline architecture was defined that would apply across missions, while allowing the flexibility to customize services. The evolution of this concept is still used today in Control Center Architecture. A generic control center architecture evolved, which scopes all the activities of a wide range of spacecraft. The use of standards both in the spacecraft system and on the ground facilitates this. The control center can be customized, essentially, by a configuration database. This works particularly well with constellations of similar or identical spacecraft. In support of constellations, we focus on the similarities, but need to track the individuality's of different units. As the constellation ages, the operational characteristics diverge. By careful trending, we can predict and perhaps prevent failures in other units.

In addition, there is an advantage to schedule and cost to developing the control center software early, and using it to support Integration and Test of the spacecraft. The biggest advantage, beyond avoiding two development efforts, is avoiding two validation activities. A huge amount of verification for each telemetry point and each command is required. Modern Control Center (software) architectures follow this approach. It also helps in training operators.

Deep Space Missions

For U. S. missions beyond the near-Earth, the responsibility falls to California Institute of Technology's Jet Propulsion Laboratory, under contract to NASA. The control center's for the various missions resemble those used at Goddard Space Flight Center for near Earth missions. They are purpose-built, since each mission is highly unique. Some JPL missions operate for decades or multiple decades, so a technology refresh is sometimes required. Their Mission control rooms are called OCC, Operations Control Centers, and the Space Flight Operations Facility, SFOF.

These rooms are a flurry of activity at launch, but can be mostly deserted during a long cruise. Then things get busy again during a planetary fly-by or landing.

With two Cubesats having gone to Mars as part of NASA's MARCO mission, the relevance of Cubesats beyond Earth is established.

Control Center Architecture, Hardware/ Software

This section discusses the hardware and software architecture of the Control Center function Basically, a Control Center needs a certain level of data communication and storage capacity, a figure that can be provided by most modern desktop and laptop machines, as well as some tablets.

Spacecraft Simulator

A good simulator is critical in the Control Center, particularly for initial checkout and for personnel training. The simulator can be developed before or concurrent with the Control Center itself, and used for validation. In operational use, the simulator can be used for anomaly investigation and to develop new scenarios. It can implemented on the same computer architecture that drives the displays and does the calculations in the control center.

It is essential that the simulator data be tagged in the header. Don't do what I did once, which was command the simulator, while wondering why the spacecraft was not responding. There's only one thing worse – commanding the spacecraft while viewing simulated data. Design this "feature" out.

A Telemetry and Command Simulator is a simple stimulus-response unit. This is adequate at a low level, but we would like to have a software spacecraft, that models dynamics, electrical power, data flow, and others. This means the simulation also has to include a lot of additional models, such as the Sun, the Earth, the moon, the star field, etc. The simulation can be evolved over time and off-the-shelf models are available for many of these functions.

Tracking

The Cubesat can be tracked by radar. NORAD, the North American Aerospace Command, based in Colorado, tracks all detectable orbital entities, from large satellites to space junk, zombie-sats, and the larger pieces of debris, as well as near-Earth asteroids.

NORAD puts all this up on a website for your convenience, in a standard format called the "two-line element" (TLE). This contains the Keplerian orbital elements, the set of data describing the orbit of anything around the Earth, for a given point in time (epoch). It is a legacy format form the 1960's, that still works. It includes two data items of 80 ASCII charters each (an IBM punch card format).

Here is the format and contents of Line 1:.

Field	Columns	Content
1	1	Line number
2	3-7	Satellite number
3	8	Classification (U = unclassified)
4	10-11	Internat. Designator, last two digits of launch year

5	12-14	Launch number of the year
6	15-17	Place of launch
7	19-20	Epoch, last two digits of year
8	21-32	Epoch, day of year, and fractional portion of day
9	34-43	First Time Derivative of the Mean Motion divided by two
10	45-52	Second Time Derivative of Mean Motion divided by six (decimal point assumed)
11	54-61	BSTAR drag term, (decimal point assumed)
12	63	number 0
13	65-68	element set number, incremented for new TLE
14	69	Checksum, modulo 19

Here is the format of line 2:

Field	Columns	Content
1	1	Line number
2	3-7	Satellite number
3	9-16	Inclination (degrees)
4	18-25	Right ascension of the ascending node (degrees)
5	27-33	Eccentricity (decimal point assumed)
6	35-42	Argument of perigee (degrees)
7	44-51	Mean Anomaly (degrees)
8	53-63	Mean Motion (revolutions per day)
9	64-68	Revolution number at epoch (revolutions)
10	69	Checksum (modulo 10)

Need your data? Get an account with spacetrack.org, and get it on line.

You can also use this service:
http://www.celestrak.com/NORAD/elements/

Need to watch out for space debris? Go here:

We should now examine frames of reference. These are 3-dimensional Newtonian references, that we can compare our spacecrafts orientation with respect to. There are many possible frames of reference, some stationary, some moving. For example, we might choose a frame at the center of the Earth, called the Earth centered (or geocentric) inertial frame. This is stationary with respect to the Earth, and we can calculate the satellite's position with respect to this frame. We can also assume the surface of the Earth rotates and wobbles a bit with respect to this frame. So, if we want to know when the spacecraft can view, say, Madrid, we calculate the position of the spacecraft and Madrid, in this frame of reference. There is also a solar-based frame, situated in the Sun. This is useful for interplanetary mission. The geocentric inertial frame moves with respect to the Sun's inertial frame. If we are in orbit around Mars, we would used a Mars-centered inertial frame. It is a similar case for the other planets. In any frame of reference, we locate the spacecraft in three dimensions, with three coordinates, x, y, z, with respect to the zero-point, or origin of the frame. It is also useful to know the spacecraft's velocity (in three dimensions) with respect to the frame. There is also a Galactic frame.

Anomaly and emergency contingency operations

In a problem scenario onboard the spacecraft, the first line of defense is the onboard computer and its software. In fact, the ground may not even be aware of the problem for hours. The onboard system has the interfaces, and, ideally, the pre-arranged solution to the problem. If transmitter A fails, turn it off, and turn on B. In the Control center, the operations team has to rely on telemetry (or the lack of it) to diagnose the problem, and come up with a procedure to fix it, and the mission. No pressure. Ideally, an inclusive list of failure scenarios have been examined, and corrective actions defined. Failing that, we have a hugely expensive, amazingly complex system in a extreme environment to diagnose and fix over a limited bandwidth link. Here, the most senior and knowledgeable operations personnel are called in to the control center. Originally, all fault repairs and workarounds would be determined in the control center, and uplinked to the spacecraft. Now, better onboard computers are tasked with the initial part of that job, with the control center as backup. There are on the scene of the problem. We will discuss the concept of self monitoring later on, in the context of Rad-Hard Software.

Engineering Tools

Various system engineering tools are available to use both before and after "incidents." Ideally, we review the systems before hand with respect to failure and safety, and factor these issues into the implementation plan. Many factors marginalize this approach, including management focus, and impact on systems cost and schedule.

After the fact, we have the Root Cause analysis method, so we can determine what exactly failed, and how this particular issue can be addressed and mitigated. In many cases, this process uncovers other latent issues that also need to be addressed. These need to be documented as case studies for the use of future projects.

Root Cause Analysis

Root Cause Analysis refers to an engineering process to identify and categorize the causes of events, and to identify the primal cause. It is a useful tool for determining why a disaster happened. It is used to define the what, how, and why (and sometimes, who)? Its value is that it will lead to a definition of corrective measures that can be applied in the future.

By definition, root causes are underlying, identifiable, and controllable. The RCA process includes a data collection phase (forensics), a cause charting, the root cause identification, recommendations, and implementation of the solution to avoid repeating the error. In many cases, the RCA will uncover other

18

failure causes that were overlooked. There are software tools available to assist in the RCA process.

Keep in mind, your solution should not introduce additional problems.

Modeling

A solar model and an atmospheric model are useful, particularly in calculating satellite lifetime. The sun is the major driver of the Earth's atmosphere, and the residual atmosphere at low Earth orbit affects spacecraft due to drag. In sunlight, the atmosphere boils up, and drag increases.

Orbit calculations can be supported in the control center, or done by a support facility. Simple modeling tools such as STK (Satellite Tool Kit) can be used. NASA-GSFC has an Open source tool called ODTBX.

Another useful thing to calculate is the ground track of the orbiting spacecraft. This is useful for coordination with ground stations, and to see a downward looking instrument's footprint.

Maintaining a thermal model of the spacecraft can lead to useful insight into thermal system performance, and can help to avoid extreme temperatures and thermal failure.

A power/energy model is useful to make sure the spacecraft batteries are always staying charged. In some cases, operations must cease until the batteries are charged.

FMEA

The failure modes and effects analysis (FMEA) is an engineering tool that is applied during the design and testing process of a system. In this approach, we postulate failure modes, and analyze their impact on the system performance. The possible failure modes are examined to confirm their validity. Then, the possible failures are prioritized by severity and consequences. The goal is to identify and eliminate failures in the order of decreasing severity.

The FMEA approach starts at the Project conceptual phase, and continue throughout the project life-cycle. It can (and should) be applied to modifications to existing projects. The origins of the FMEA approach were during World War-II, by the U. S. Military. After the war, the approach was adopted by the aviation and automotive industries.

The FMEA analysis requires a cross-functional team, consisting, as applicable of hardware and software engineers, manufacturing, Quality Assurance, test engineers, reliability engineers, parts engineers, and, ideally, the customer.

The process involves identifying the scope of the project, defining the boundaries and the desired level of detail. Then, the system (or project) functions are identified. Each function is analyzed to identify how it could fail. For each of these failure cases, the consequences are noted. These range from no effects to catastrophic. Formally, the consequences are rated on a scale of 1 to 10, with 1 being insignificant to 10, catastrophic. The root cause is then determined for each consequence, starting with the 10's. Software tools are available to support this analysis process.

Once the causes are determined, the controls are defined. Controls prevent the cause from happening, reduce the probability of happening, or detect the failure in time for correction to be applied. For each control, then, a detection probability rating is calculated (or estimated), again on a scale of 1-10. Here, 1 indicates that control is certain, and 10 indicates that the solution will not work. By definition, critical characteristics of the system have a severity of 9 or greater, and have an occurrence and detection rating of greater than 3.

A Risk Priority Number (RPN) is calculated, which is severity times occurrence time detection (ratings). This measure is used to rank failure modes in the order in which they are to be addressed. Of course, some of these rankings are not measurable, but the result of good engineering guesses. From an FMEA, you can develop contingency plans, adjust to the identified failure scenarios. It is always good to have a Plan B. Also C, D, E......

FMEA's apply to Mission Operations as well as to the spacecraft.

Fault Tree

A fault tree is a graphical representation of faults and their causes. It provides a top-down deductive analysis for a system. There are software tools to facilitate the construction of the tree, which just allows you to visualize binary decision points. It must be complete (full fault coverage) and correct.

Fault Tolerance

Fault tolerance refers to the feature of a system that allows for certain faults or certain sequences of faults to not affect operation or safety. The system might be said to be capable of graceful degradation. Obviously, there is a limit to how many faults the system can survive, and many faults cause subsequent ripple-effects. Loss of attitude control causes a shortage of power, which causes communication to be lost...

A defective design can be identified and corrected before it leads to an accident thanks to quality assurance and analysis of flight parameters during testing and operation of any space hardware. This is where complacency comes into play. Failures involving complex systems are always preceded by so-called accident precursors, which take the form of parameters out of tolerance. People responsible for those systems become accustomed to the idea that nothing bad will ever happen because nothing bad has happened yet.

21

Fault Containment

Fault Containment means we might have a fault, but it can be contained or isolated locally. This minimize the impact of the fault, and keep it from getting worse. Opportunities for fault containment are in the design phase, after a good FMEA has been done. Then, the systems can be analyzed with a goal of minimizing subsequent faults and failures.

Mitigation

Fault mitigation means you have designed the system with what we might call reflex actions in response to a detected fault, and healing actions, that offset the failure. This can't be done across all faults, but an evaluation of the system with various what-if scenarios, may allow for automatic responses to faults.

BIST

Built-in self-test is part of the design-for-testability philosophy. It is applicable at the box, board, or chip level. It defines the inclusion of additional circuitry or code specifically for testing purposes. It will include software components. For example, when a standard pc system is reset, the initial code performs a series of functional tests on the hardware of the board hardware. This is generally referred to as POST – Power-On-Self-Test. The validity of command and telemetry data bases should also be checked. This could be done with a checksum over the database. Besides onboard use, BIST is a good approach for the control center host machine(s).

Remote Maintenance and troubleshooting

Once you have secured the Control Center, it can be prepared for remote debugging, letting the cognizant personnel in through the firewall. This relieves the facility from having to have troubleshooters deployed 24x7. If you have hosted the facility "in the cloud" this service comes along with the hosting.

Mission planning & scheduling

A major activity in the Control Center involves mission planning and scheduling of resources. This results in a daily time-line of activities. Contingency plans and re-plans are also produced. The Mission plans are very detailed, and there is usually one or more mission planners full time. No good plan "they say" survives first contact with reality.

Flight dynamics tools

Flight Dynamics includes attitude and orbit determination and control. GSFC's General Mission Analysis Tool (GMAT) is available as free and open source software, under the NASA Open Source Agreement. The tool provides the ability to model and optimize spacecraft trajectories and orbits. The domain can be LEO, lunar, interplanetary, or deep space.

The spacecraft has to know its orientation with respect to an inertial frame of reference. We use the word "orbit" to describe the spacecraft's position and velocity. It used to be the case that a separate facility would use the tracking data to calculate the orbital parameters, and forward these to the Control Center. Later, the Control Centers generally took over this function. We need not only the parameters of the orbit as its exists now, but what it will be in the future. This is the function of orbit propagation. We are limited in how far into the future we can predict the orbit, due to data limitations, perturbations that affect the spacecraft, and not having a closed form solution.

If the spacecraft uses magnetic torquer bars to push against the Earth's magnetic field for attitude adjustment or momentum unloading, we need a map of the Earth's magnetic field onboard, particularly, the orientation of magnetic north to "north" in the inertial frame of reference.

Generally, the attitude of a spacecraft is described as a vector in a frame of reference that is body-centered in the spacecraft. We can use three rotational parameters to describe the spacecraft's attitude with respect to this frame. These are generally referred to as roll, pitch, and yaw, derived from aircraft. Keep in mind, the body-centric frame we are using is moving with the spacecraft, relative to the Earth Centered frame. We use Newtonian rigid-body dynamics to model the system. This is a good approximation, unless the spacecraft does not act as a rigid body.

Roll indicates a rotation about the velocity vector, the direction of motion. *Pitch* is a rotation up and down, with respect to the velocity vector. *Yaw* is a left-right rotation with respect to the velocity vector. It makes more sense in an aircraft, with wings.

We should mention Euler angles. These are used to describe the rotation of an object with respect to a rigid frame of reference. If we use the spacecraft body-centric frame, the Euler angles correspond to roll, pitch, and yaw.

There is another entity that is sometimes used for attitude, called quaternions. These are 4-unit vectors (as opposed to 3-unit roll-pitch-yaw), so they contain redundant orientation, but are a little easier to calculate, Keep in mind, we can rotate in 2 or 3 directions at the same time. So, quaternions, invented in 1843, are used to calculate and describe complex three dimensional rotations.

Essentially, the quaternion is a vector in the inertial space, pointing in a direction described by the dimensions along the three axes. Then, a fourth parameter describes a rotation around that vector.

It is fairly easy to translate from quaternions back and forth to Euler angles. This is left as an exercise for the student.

If the orbit of the spacecraft is below that of the GPS satellites, it can use the GPS data for position and orientation information, the same as we do on the surface of the Earth. The constellation of GPS satellites orbits at slightly more than 20,000 kilometers, and thus serves the LEO community. An off-the-shelf GPS unit intended for surface usage will need some modifications to work in orbit. Specifically, the ionosphere correction factors need to be removed.

Training

A major role of the Control Center is to train operations personnel. Before launch, and during periods when the spacecraft is not in view of a ground station, the control center can use a spacecraft software-based simulator for training and practice for both normal and contingency situations.

Off-line analysis & trending; performance assessment

One role that is done in the Control Center's "back-room" is analysis and trending of the telemetry data. This is not a real-time task, and can be done as a background task. This leads to assessments of the spacecraft subsystems performance, and identifies trends, such as battery degradation and decreased thermal performance. These are usually gradual effects, and don't require up-to-the-moment real-time attention.

NASA-GSFC's Integrated Trending and Plotting (ITP) tool is an example. It implements data retrieval, filtering, and reporting functions. It has a remote web interface, and is PC-based.

Calibration is another engineering task, As the mission goes progresses, equipment ages, and previously calibration curves derived from testing need updating.

Data Archiving

Data archiving of all incoming data is done in the control center, although this now uses COTS database tools. Off-site data repository's in the Cloud may be used. It is important to have sufficient workstations in the control center to allow playback of archived telemetry during real time operations if desired.

Support I&T

The same Control Center that will support the Mission can be used earlier to support Integration and Test. Not all of the functionality is required at this stage. The advantages of this approach are that the Control Center software and databases will be validated, the operations team can gain experience, and the system can be evolved, using lessons-learned. Keep in mind, the primary users during the I&T phase are test engineers, not Operations Personnel. This approach also avoids a dual develop effort. The test support configuration evolves into the control center configuration.

Science Data Processing

Generally, science (instrument) data is stripped out in the control center, and sent to a specialized science data processing data. It is common for it to be archived with all other telemetry in the control center, but there will also be a dedicated science data archive. Most of the time, quick-look capability is provided for science data in the control center.

Definition of data Processing Levels

NASA Earth Data products are processed at various levels ranging from Level 0 to Level 4. Level 0 products are raw data at full instrument resolution. At higher levels, the data are converted into more useful parameters and formats. Instruments may produce data at any of these levels. This is the domain of NASA's Earth Observing System Data and Information System (EOSDIS), a large data processing facility dedicated to Earth Science at GSFC.

Data Level 0
Reconstructed, unprocessed instrument and payload data at full resolution, with any and all communications artifacts (erg., synchronization frames, communications headers, duplicate data) removed. In most cases, the EOS Data and Operations System (EDOS) provides these data to the data centers as production data sets for processing by the Science Data Processing Segment (SDPS) or by a SIPS to produce higher-level products.

Data Level 1A

This is reconstructed, unprocessed instrument data at full resolution, time-referenced, and annotated with ancillary information, including radiometric and geometric calibration coefficients and ego-referencing parameters (erg., platform ephemeris) computed and appended but not applied to Level 0 data.

Data Level 1B
This is Level 1A data that have been processed to sensor units (not all instruments have Level 1B source data).

Data Level 3
This is variables mapped on uniform space-time grid scales, usually with some completeness and consistency.

Data Level 4
Model output or results from analyses of lower-level data (erg., variables derived from multiple measurements).

Early orbit checkout.

The Cubesat is launched powered-off, and needs to remain radio-silent for a short period after deployment. The first communication gives an indication of aliveness – the Cubesat survived the launch environment. The first data items are critical.

It may not be possible to monitor the initial telemetry in real time. Generally, the Cubesats communicate via ground terminals, and the deployment may be over water. This increase the ground-side stress levels.

The Control Center is the primary user gateway to the spacecraft. It may generate the data products for the end users of the system. In the engineering case, this is the downlinked spacecraft health and status information. The spacecraft is carrying one or more science instruments, and this data is usually passed along to a science data processing and archive center. There can be a high level of automation for routine operations, like scheduled updates, and more directed operations for anomalies. An example of a routine operation that can easily be automated is consumables tracking.

Multiple Control Centers provide redundancy and geographical diversity. It is possible to have a generic Control Center, that is software configurable for different missions on demand. This depends heavily on flexibility of the configuration, and adherence to standards.

Constellation support

In many cases, the satellite control center handles a constellation of multiple spacecraft. This includes the GPS constellation, the weather satellite systems, TDRSS, and a number of commercial communications satellites, providing data service world-wide. An emerging concept is constellations of Cubesats. An Constellation of 50 2U and 3U Cubesats was deployed in 2015. Some were released from the ISS, and some from a rocket launch. They collected and telemetered data on the lower thermospere. This is not a Constellation, per se, but 50 units acting on their own, reporting back to their home institutions. Universities around the world participated, and built units from the QB50 specification

Managing a constellation adds to the complexity. Even if each spacecraft is built to the same plan, different spacecraft, launched at different times, and having differing times on-orbit, need customized attention. The most important aspect is to have a unique identifier, so you know which spacecraft you're talking or listening to.

An approach to Constellation control centers can involve a hierarchy of a master control center with multiple space assets to control, or a peer network of individual control centers, that also provides built-in redundancy and backup. A backup control center

28

is useful not only for anomalies at the primary center, but also to allow for maintenance and upgrade of the primary center, and for personnel training and certification.

An ongoing debate in the optimum architecture for multi-satellite control is between a centralized design, and a distributed architecture. Centralized is the legacy approach. Distributed takes advantage of advances in networking and abstraction. In the distributed approach, multiple ground stations and control centers are linked by existing terrestrial data communication resources.

The distributed architecture scales more freely, with computation, storage, and communications resources being added as demand increases. High system reliability and security can be maintained from industry best practices. The scalable, distributed technology has been driven by large data-centric organizes such as Google, and retailers such as Amazon, as well as social media sites such as Facebook and Utube. These do not meet military-grade security, of course, but that can be addressed.

Another advantage of the distributed approach is dynamic allocation of resources, having (and paying for) resources when you need them, not all the time. The system provides mission safety simultaneously with cost effectiveness. A metric of interest is the staff to spacecraft ratio. If domain-skilled staff can be shared among the constellation, yet be brought together in the case of anomalies, personnel costs can be contained. Distributed approaches provide economy of scale.

The same information for each spacecraft in a homogeneous constellations provides summaries of critical cross-platform information. If we just had a failure on one spacecraft, we will look for that to happen on others. A merged database, allows for trending information to flow forward. As constellations age, the individual members age and fail at different rates. From trending data on early failures, the remaining spacecraft can be monitored especially for known failures and degradation.

The T&C handbook

The Telemetry & Command Handbook is a crucial document for the Control Center. It contains and defines each command, and each telemetry point for the uplink and downlink. It is now commonly a database. Compiling the T&C handbook begins early in the project, and continues to be updated during flight. It is desirable to keep the Handbook in electronic form, under configuration control.

Ground Segment

The Ground Segment consists of the antennas, RF receivers and transmitters, and communication lines to the Control Center. The Ground segment is the link between the control center, and the satellites. All data are archived at the ground segment, in case of communication interruption with the control center.

Near-Earth Network

The Near Earth Network (NEN) communicates with near-Earth orbiting satellites (out to Lunar orbit). It uses the NASA ground stations. There are two stations in Florida, in proximity to the Kennedy Center launch site, at the launch facility at Wallops Island, Virginia, and at the McMurdo Base in Antarctica. In addition, other commercial ground stations can be used, under contract to NASA. Goddard Space Flight Center in Greenbelt, Maryland, manages the NEN, which was formally know as the Ground Network (GN). The dish antennae of the GN range from 34 meters to 70 meters in diameter. Non-NASA users can arrange to use the NeN on a non-interference basis, but it is expensive.

Space Network

The Space Network (SN) dates back to the early 1980's, when NASA introduced a constellation of satellites to replace the ground tracking stations.

The Tracking and Data Relay Satellites, in geosynchronous orbit, are the Space Segment (SS) of the SN. They implement communications between to low Earth orbiting spacecraft , and one of the TDRSS ground segments. The ground segment units are located at White Sands, New Mexico, and on Guam Island, in the Pacific. White Sands also serves as the controlling station for the TDRS spacecraft. The TDRS network was declared operational in 1989. STDN stations at Wallops island, Bermuda, Merritt Island (FL), Ponce de Leon (FL), and Dakar, Senegal, remained operational.

The Tracking & Data Relay Satellite System is over 30 years old, and is being refreshed with new technology. The Space Segment has spare assets in orbit in case of failure. Non-NASA Cubesats do not currently use the SN, due to cost.

Deep Space Network

NASA's Deep Space Network consists of three sites spaced around the planet. It supports deep space missions for NASA and other entities. It is managed by the Jet Propulsion Lab (JPL) in Pasadena, California.. The nearest station to JPL is at Goldstone, in the desert to the east. Two other stations, in Spain and Australia are spaced about 120 degrees apart on the globe from Goldstone. The DSN started operations in the 1960's, with teletype communications with the Pasadena facility. The DSN is heavily used, but can provide backup to the Space Network for contingencies. The SN can support NASA's interplanetary missions. The Deep Space Network is over-booked just for NASA missions. As planetary Cubesat missions evolve, new approaches to T&C support will be needed. Optical communications is being considered by JPL.

Cubesat T&C

Cubesats are generally low cost, University-class missions and the Cubesat community needs low cost telemetry and command support. One approach is provided by Satnogs (satnogs.org), which is a low cost, cooperative satellite ground station network. It uses a modular architecture, with a global management architecture that allows for remote operation of multiple, geographically-dispersed ground stations. It is based on open source hardware and software.

There is a large number of compatible ground stations around the world, operated by schools or individuals. These are all tied together, over the Internet. Each agrees to handle each other's telemetry and commanding. An example installation is at MakerFaire in New York. It features a yagi antenna for 144.8 MHz, and a helical antenna for 437 MHz.

The Satnogs website provides all the information for building the necessary antenna, the ground receiver, and the Internet connection, as well as the software. The tracking system for the antennas is 3-D printable, and driven by stepper motors. The baseline configuration includes the BeagleBone Black or the TP-Link TL-WR703N ($25.) single-board computer. Running Debian Linux or OpenWrt, it supports all ground station functionality (status, tracking, signal receiving and processing) over LAN or WiFi for extreme mobility or remote operation. (https://satnogs.org)

Onboard command receivers and telemetry transmitters can use common Software Defined Radio techniques. The Raspberry Pi is capable of providing these services, at the 433 MHz level.

NASA provides telemetry and command support for its own Cubesat missions, using its existing Near Earth Network and Space Network (TDRSS). The agency is planning to support lunar, L1/L2, and Mars mission.

An Amateur radio operator's license is required from your home country for the Cubesat to include a transmitter, and for the ground station. In the U.S., this is handled by the FCC. Generally, the Cubesat uplink/downlink is 433 MHz, which can be handled with Software Defined Radio (SDR) code in something like a Raspberry

Pi.

UHF and VHF off-the-shelf transceivers for Cubesats are available commercially. There are also some S-band units, using patch antennas. Deployable antennas are allowed, and used for the lower frequencies. The higher the frequency, the greater the downlink bandwidth can be. There is also an impact on solar array size, due to greater downlink power.

It is also possible for a Cubesat to use the Globalstar satellite constellation for continuous communication to and from the ground. The radio unit is off-the-shelf. There are 40 Globalstar satellites in 1,400 km Earth orbit, and 14 ground stations. Data plan rates can be an issue, but start at around $40. At the moment, data is handled in 15 second bundles. Data is handled in SMS format, or 9,600 bps packets.

Infrastructure

This section discusses the support structure for the mission control center. This includes the computation and communication assets. A reliable source of power is also essential. For 24x7 operation, such as required in early on-orbit checkout, human needs must be considered, such as a snack bar, and places to catch a quick nap.

The incoming telemetry data and the outgoing uplink commands use serial data links to and from the control center, to an antenna facility. The command (uplink) rate is generally low and usually infrequent.

Security

The Control Center has issues of security, both operational and data. First, it needs to be a controlled access facility. Only authorized personnel should be in the Control Center facility But don't forget virtual users. Can the control center computers be hacked into? What ports and backdoors exist in the implementation? Best practices from the Computer/Network

Security Industry should be applied. Lose your laptop, lose your Cubesat.

The Control Center must quickly act quickly to identify and react to counterattacks. These might be phishing expeditions to steal data, malicious attacks to gain control of space assets, or denial of service attacks. A good penetration-testing of the facility should be conducted. There should be a permanent Security Officer, with the responsibility for data and operations.

Open Source versus Proprietary

This is a topic we need to discuss before we get very far into software. It is not a technical topic, but concerns your right to use (and/or own, modify) software. It's those software licenses you click to agree with, and never read. That's what the intellectual property lawyers are betting on.

Software and software tools are available in proprietary and open source versions. Open source software is free and widely available, and may be incorporated into your system. It is available under license, which generally says that you can use it, but derivative products must be made available under the same license. This presents a problem if it is mixed with purchased, licensed commercial software, or a level of exclusivity is required. Major government agencies such as the Department of Defense and NASA have policies related to the use of Open Source software.

Adapting a commercial or open source operating system to a particular problem domain can be tricky. Usually, the commercial operating systems need to be used "as-is" and the source code is not available. The software can usually be configured between well-defined limits, but there will be no visibility of the internal workings. For the open source situation, there will be a multitude of source code modules and libraries that can be configured and customized, but the process is complex. The user can also write new modules in this case.

Large corporations or government agencies sometimes have problems incorporating open source products into their projects. Open Source did not fit the model of how they have done business traditionally. They are issues and lingering doubts. Many Federal agencies have developed Open Source policies. NASA has created an open source license, the NASA Open Source Agreement (NOSA), to address these issues. It has released software under this license, but the Free Software Foundation had some issues with the terms of the license. The Open Source Initiative (www.opensource.org) maintains the definition of Open Source, and certifies licenses such as the NOSA.

The GNU General Public License (GPL) is the most widely used free software license. It guarantees end users the freedoms to use, study, share, copy, and modify the software. Software that ensures that these rights are retained is called free software. The license was originally written by Richard Stallman of the Free Software Foundation (FSF) for the GNU project in 1989. The GPL is a *copyleft* license, which means that derived works can only be distributed under the same license terms. This is in distinction to permissive free software licenses, of which the BSD licenses are the standard examples. Copyleft is in counterpoint to traditional copyright. Proprietary software "poisons" free software, and cannot be included or integrated with it, without abandoned the GPL. The GPL covers the GNU/linux operating systems and most of the GNU/linux-based applications.

A Vendor's software tools and operating system or application code is usually proprietary intellectual property. It is unusual to get the source code to examine, at least without binding legal documents and additional funds. Along with this, you do get the vendor support. An alternative is open source code, which is in the public domain. There are a series of licenses covering open source code usage, including the Creative Commons License, the gnu public license, copyleft, and others. Open Source describes a collaborative environment for development and testing. Use of open source code carries with it an implied responsibility to "pay back" to the community. Open Source is not necessarily free.

The Open source philosophy is sometimes at odds with the rigidized procedures evolved to ensure software performance and reliability. Offsetting this is the increased visibility into the internals of the software packages, and control over the entire software package. Besides application code, operating systems such as GNU/linux and bsd can be open source. The programming language Python is open source. The popular web server Apache is also open source.

ITAR

Systems that provide "satellite control software" are included under the International Trafficking in Arms (ITAR) regulation, as the software is defined as "munitions" subject to export control. The Department of State interprets and enforces ITAR regulations. It applies to items that might go to non-US citizens, even citizens of friendly nations or NATO Partners. Even items received from Allies may not necessarily be provided back to them. Software and embedded systems related to launch vehicles and satellites are given particular scrutiny. The ITAR regulations date from the period of the Cold War with the Soviet Union. Increased enforcement of ITAR regulations recently have resulted in American market share in satellite technology declining. A license is required to export controlled technology. This includes passing technical information to a foreign national within the United States. Penalties of up to $100 million have been imposed for violations of the ITAR Regulations, and imprisonment is also possible. Something as simple as carrying ITAR information on a laptop or storage medium outside the US is considered a violation. ITAR regulations are complex, and need to be understood when working in areas of possible application. ITAR regulations apply to the hardware, software, and Intellectual Property assets, as well as test data and documentation.

Internet, and IoT

The Internet is a global data highway, and there is even an Interplanetary Internet. The concept dates from early efforts in data transmission in the 1970's, and works quite well. Satellite data can be collected at any downlink station, and sent to a satellite control center over the Internet. Similarly, commands can be sent for uplink. Similarly, uplinks to the spacecraft can be transmitted over the Internet, with proper security protocols in place. Data privacy may also be a concern. The Internet uses TCP/IP protocols, and spacecraft generally use CCSDS protocols.

The Internet grew out of the DoD sponsored ARPAnet, which was modeled on AlohaNet, invented to allow data communications among the Hawaii Islands.

Packets are bundled data, handled identically by the transmission system. Think of them as containers of data, in the same way that standardized containerized freight revolutionized global freight delivery. The standard container is compatible with rail, road, and water transportation. The packet, with its data content moves by radio, or optical fiber, landline, satellite link, and more. Besides the information ("payload"), the packet contains control information such as receiver address, sender address, packet number (for payloads spread across packets), possibly error detection and correction information, etc. In the seven layer network model, packets are data units at level three. The data payload of a packet can be variable length.

CCSDS Packets are used on near-Earth and Deep Space communication links. These have more rigorous error detection and correction schemes. The data length is variable, and can be from 7 to 65,542 bytes, which includes the header. Packet sizes are fixed length. The transmission of packets is via data frames, which are also fixed length. The frame also contains control information. The data frames are the legacy component of the space communication segment.

We can have universal world-wide connectivity, using the .net framework, which is free and open source software. Net framework allows a device to be a http client. It can access data, provide data, and access services. It handles the hard part with code for requests and the socket interface, and is available as off-the-shelf libraries. It is also available per-programmed into flash memory, and provides access to a huge ecosystem of network resources.

So now, not only people with desktops, laptops, tablets and phone can populate the Internet, along with the server/cloud architecture, but devices can as well. This concept of IoT kicked off around 2014, but has seen tremendous growth. It is estimated that there are more "things" on the Internet, than people. These are event driven. There is some concern this whole structure will become non-deterministic, even practically. It's just too complex, and feeding upon itself. The applications are limited only by imagination. Cubesats and their monitoring and control centers can be items on the IoT.

We need to architect and implement the IoT carefully. At least as long as we are in charge. It can provide a whole new world-wide platform for cyber-attacks. How can it be managed? Can it be managed? It is a rapidly evolving system, with positive feedback. There are privacy concerns. Now that this is working, we can't put the Genie back in the bottle. We can only hold on, and hope to steer. Does the Internet of Things really need us?

The Internet of Things is built upon web-accessible embedded systems. More and more embedded systems are on the web. This allows to integrate cheap embedded devices with ubiquitous web services, accessible with wireless technologies. An example is a smart electric meters. Smart devices, including satellites, can access data, provide data, or access services.

To make use of this concept, we need uniquely identifiable objects such as smart sensors, smart actuators, smart platforms. What is the identity scheme? The Uniform Resource Locator (URL) approach can be adopted We also need advanced connectivity to the Internet, which provides distance-insensitive world-wide connectivity. These are large areas of the Earth's surface where the Internet does not reach, but satellite links can be used, although this is an expensive approach. The polar regions enjoy good satellite communications due to a series of polar orbiting spacecraft.

There are now be more "things" on the Internet than people. Cubesats are "things." There is a huge ecosystem of devices, talking to cloud servers, and among themselves. This reduce the reliance on people (who needs us anyway?).

Cloud servers allow access to "unlimited" datasets and resources. The latest trend is cloud robotics, where a connected mobile platform can offload computational and storage resources by having a good communications link.

Free and open source software and collaborative development environments enhance the deployment process. There are standard software interfaces for communication protocols.

File Systems

A file system provides a way to organize data in a standard format. The file system stores the data, and metadata (data about the data) such as date, time, permissions, etc. Some operating systems support multiple file systems.

The important thing to keep in mind about about a file systems is, don't reinvent the wheel! There are many good file systems out there, and the provide a compatibility across platforms. Most are based on the original disk operating system (dos) model.

The legacy DOS file structure is built upon linked lists. The directory file contains lists of files and information about them. It uses a 32-byte entry per file, containing the file name, extension, attributes, date and time, and the starting location of the file on disk.

The File Allocation Table (FAT) is a built map of allocated clusters on the disk. A cluster is the default unit of storage. It's size is a trade-off between efficiency of storage, and efficiency of access. A size of 256 bytes to 1024 bytes worked well in the early days. Two copies of the FAT are kept by the system, and these are on fixed locations of the storage media.

A directory file has entries for all of the files on the disk. The name of the file is in 8.3 format, meaning an 8 character file name, and a 3-character extension. The extension tells the type of the file, executable program, word processing, etc. By DOS convention, when a file is erased, the first character of the name is changed to the Hex character E5. The data is not lost at this point. If nothing else happens in the mean-time, the file can be un-erased, and recovered. However, the E5 signifies the space the file occupied is now available for use.

Various file attribute bits are kept. The file can be marked as read-only, hidden, reserved system type, and bits indicate a directory field, a volume label (name of a storage volume, like, "disk1"), and whether the file has been archived (saved). There is a 16-bit date code in the format (year-1980)*512 + month * 32 + day. (thought exercise – when do we have a problem?). The starting cluster number in a directory is kept as a word value. This limits us to 216 clusters.

Linux supports it own file systems formats, ext3 and 4, as well as FAT.

Databases

Databases are useful for organizing data, and making it easy to access. The are many excellent database products, usually based on the Structured Query Language (SQL) model. The incoming telemetry and outgoing commands are stored, time tagged. There is no need to re-invent the wheel again here. Commercial databases (and some come in open source versions) scale well and provide the security and query features needed. SQL is the linux-based product of choice, with the SQLlite slimmed down version applicable to spacecraft onboard use.

Standards

There are many Standards applicable to Cubesats. Why should we be interested in standards? Standards represent an established approach, based on best practices. Standards are not created to stifle creativity or define an implementation approach, but rather to capture the benefits of previous experience. Adherence to standards implies that different parts will work together. Standards are often developed by a single company, and then adopted by the relevant industry. Other standards are mandated by large customer organizations such as the Department of Defense, or NASA. Many standards organizations exist to develop, review, and maintain standards.

Standards exist in many areas, including hardware, software, interfaces, protocols, testing, system safety, security, and certification. Standards can be open or closed (proprietary).

Hardware standards include the form factor and packaging of chips, the electrical interface, the bus interface, the power interface, and others. The JTAG standard specifies an interface for debugging.

In computers, the Instruction set architecture (ISA) specifies the instruction set. It does not specify the implementation. A popular ISA is ARM (ARM Holdings, LTD), used for Raspberry Pi and Arduino. These are proprietary, and licensed by the Intellectual Property holder to chip manufacturers.

In software, an API (applications program interface) specifies the interface between a user program, and the operating system. To run properly, the program must adhere to the API.

Language standards also exist, such as those for the ANSI c and Java languages. Networking standards include TCP/IP for Ethernet, the CAN bus from Bosch, IEEE-1553 for avionics, and USB.

It is always good to review what standards are available and could be applied to a system, as it ensures the application of best practices from experience, and interoperability with other systems.

ARINC 653 is a software specification (API) for space and time partitioning in safety critical real-time operating systems. Each piece of application software has its own memory and dedicated time slot. The specification dates from 1996.

The Consultive Committee for Space Data Standards, (CCSDS),. maintains International standards that covers system engineering, space link, space-internetworking, and onboard interfaces. The CCSDS is made up of 11 member nations, and over 750 missions have used these.

Why don't we just use good old TCP/IP? Transmission Control Protocol/Internet Protocol was designed for terrestrial usage. It assumes end-end connectivity, and low delays. It focuses on speed and simplicity. Space communications can be long-delay. IP assumes seamless, end-end, available data path. Some of the newer mobile IP protocols more closely address the space environment.

The use of Internet Protocol for space missions is a convenience, and piggy-backs on the large established infrastructure of terrestrial data traffic. However, there are problems. A variation of mobile IP is used, because the spacecraft might not always be in view of a ground station, and traffic through the Tracking and Data Relay Satellites involves a significant delay. A hand off scheme between various "cell" sites must be used, and a delay-tolerant protocol.

The formalized Interplanetary Internet evolved from a study at JPL, lead by Internet pioneer Vint Cerf, and Adrian Hook, from the CCSDS group. The concepts evolved to address very long delay and variable delay in communications links. For example, the Earth to Mars delay varies depending on where each planet is located in its orbit around the Sun. For some periods, one planet is behind the Sun from the point of view of the other, and communications between them is impossible for days and weeks. The Interplanetary Internet implements a Bundle Protocol to address large and variable delays. Normal IP traffic assumes a seamless, end-to-end, available data path, without worrying about the physical mechanism. The Bundle protocol addresses the case of high probability of errors, and disconnections. This protocol was tested in communication with an Earth orbiting satellite in 2008

The CCSDS, Consultive Committee on Space Data Standards, has evolved a delay tolerant protocol for use in space. A concept called the Interplanetary Internet uses a store-and-forward node in orbit around a planet (initially, Mars) that would burst-transmit data back to Earth during available communications windows. At certain times, when the geometry is right, the Mars bound traffic might encounter significant interference. Mars surface craft communicate to Orbiters, which relay the transmissions to Earth. This allows for a lower wattage transmitter on the surface vehicle. Mars does not (yet) have the full infrastructure that is currently in place around the Earth – a network of navigation, weather, and communications satellites.

The Cubesat Space Protocol is a network layer protocol, specifically for Cubesats, released in 2010 It features a 32-bit header with both network layer and transport layer data. It is written in the c language, and works with linux and FreeRTOS. The protocol and its implementation is Open source. At the physical layer, the protocol supports CAN bus, I2C, RS-232, TCP/IP, and CCDSDS space link protocol.

In space, we can use FTP over CCSDS, but watch those NAK's. When you send a packet and receive a negative acknowledgment (NAK), you usually resend. Too many negative acknowledgments can overload the capacity of the link. There is a defined and Interplanetary Internet, which address long delays, major error sources. It uses store-and-forward (like the Internet) nodes in orbit around a planet., such as Mars. It uses burst transmission back to Earth. It is a bundle protocol, assuming a high probability of errors and a non-continuous link. This is a JPL Project.

Interplanetary Internet

Communications between planets in our solar system involves long distances, and significant delay. New protocols are needed to address the long delay times, and error sources.

A concept called the Interplanetary Internet uses a store-and-forward node in orbit around a planet (initially, Mars) that burst-transmits data back to Earth during available communications windows. At certain times, when the geometry is right, the Mars bound traffic might encounter significant interference. Mars surface craft communicate to Orbiters, which relay the transmissions to Earth. This allows for a lower wattage transmitter on the surface vehicle.

For satellites in near Earth orbit, protocols based on the cellular terrestrial network can be used, because the delays are small. In fact, the International Space Station is a node on the Internet. By the time you get to the moon, it takes about a second and a quarter for electromagnetic energy to traverse the distance. Delay tolerant protocols were developed for mobile terrestrial communication, but break down in very long delay situations.

We have a good communications model and a lot of experience in Internet communications. One of the first implementations for space used a File Transfer Protocol (FPP) running over the CCSDS space communications protocol in 1996.

The formalized Interplanetary Internet evolved from a study at

JPL, lead by Internet pioneer Vint Cerf, and Adrian Hook, from the CCSDS group. The concepts evolved to address very long delay and variable delay in communications links. For example, the Earth to Mars delay varies depending on where each planet is located in its orbit around the Sun. For some periods, one planet is behind the Sun from the point of view of the other, and communications between them is impossible for days and weeks.

The Interplanetary Internet implements a Bundle Protocol to address large and variable delays. Normal IP traffic assumes a seamless, end-to-end, available data path, without worrying about the physical mechanism. The Bundle protocol addresses the cases of high probability of errors, and disconnections. This protocol was tested in communication with an Earth orbiting satellite in 2008

Fault Tolerant Design

In this design approach, a system is designed to continue to operate properly in the event of one or more failures. It is sometimes referred to as graceful degradation. There is, of course, a limit to the number of faults or failures than can be handled, and the faults or failures may not be independent. Sometimes, the system will be designed to degrade, but not fail, as a result of the fault. Fault recovery in a fault-tolerate design is either roll forward, or roll back. Roll back refers to returning the system state to a previous check-pointed state. Roll forward corrects the current system state to allow continuation. Can you recover your platform if it fails, or will it be at the bottom of a lake, or achieving terminal velocity as it falls through the atmosphere (toward your neighbor's dog house)?

Redundancy

Redundancy refers to the technique of having multiple copies of critical components. This applies equally to hardware or software. This approach increases the reliability of the system. Redundant units can be deployed in parallel, such as extra structural members, where each single unit can handle the load. This

45

provides what is referred to as a margin of safety. An improvement in reliability can be achieved by simply adding a second unit in many cases. In certain systems that are responsible for safety-critical tasks, we might triplicate the critical portion, which, reduces the probability of system failure to small, acceptable, levels.

Of course, if there is a common error in the three units, we have not increased our reliability. This situation is referred to as a common mode or single point error. Another problem is in the voting logic, that makes the decision that an error has been made, and switches controllers. At least one satellite launch failed because the voting logic made the wrong choice. Redundancy carries penalties in size, power, cost, and testing complexity, all of which affect the design.

Fault isolation allows the system to operate around the failed component, using backup or alternative modules. Fault containment strives to isolate the fault, and prevent propagation of the failure.

Systems can be designed to be fail-safe, fail-soft, or can be "melt-before-fail." The more fault tolerance that is built into a system, the more it will cost, and the more difficult it will be to test. It is important not to increase the complexity to the point where the system is not testable, and is "designed to fail." Geographic diversity is important to support of ongoing missions. This no longer requires multiple physical implementations. If the control center is virtualized, then a hosting provider can have multiple instances of the control center synchronized and running at geographically diverse locations.

Control Center Security

Has your satellite been hacked yet? Is your satellite data being used by others without your permission? Are you sure?

Every system has aspects of security. Satellite control centers operate in a hostile world. They are vulnerable to variations of hacking, viruses and malware, theft, damage, spoofing, and other nasty techniques from the desktop/server world. GPS systems can be hacked to provide incorrect location or critical time information. A bored teenage hacker in Europe took over the city Tram system as his private full-scale railroad, using a TV remote. What about the teenager in an internet café is a third-world country. Can he or she take over and play with your satellite? Yes, anytime they want to.

Some of these issues are addressed by existing protocols and standards for access and communications security. Security may also imply system stability and availability. Standard security measures such as security reviews and audits, threat analyses, target and threat assessments, countermeasures deployment, and extensive testing apply to the control center.

The completed functional system may need additional security features, such as intrusion detection, data encryption, and other features that are used in large computer installations and network facilities for Industry.

Virus and malware attacks on desktops and servers are common, and an entire industry related to detection, prevention, and correction has been spawned. Attacks on new technology such as cell phones, pda's, tablets, and GPS systems have happened. Not all of the threats come from individuals. Some are large government-funded efforts or commercial entities seeking proprietary information or market position. Security breaches can be inspired by ideology, money, or fame considerations. The *CERT* (Computer Emergency Response Team) organization at Carnegie Mellon University, and the *SANS Institute* (SysAdmin, Audit, Networking, and Security) track security incidents.

Techniques such as hard checksums and serial numbers are one approach to device protection. If unused computer ports exist, the corresponding device drivers should be disabled, or not included. Mechanisms built into the cpu hardware can provide protection of system resources such as memory.

Security has to be designed in from the very beginning; it can't just be added on. Memorize this. There will be a quiz.

Even the most innocuous platform can be used as a springboard to penetrate other systems. It is essential to consider security of all embedded systems, be aware of industry best practices and lessons learned, and use professional help in this specialized area. Virtualization can enhance or detract from security.

Control Center I/O

The satellite control center receives spacecraft telemetry and tracking information, and sends commands to the spacecraft. Nowadays, command and telemetry data mostly travels on the Internet.

Open Source tools for the Control Center

A list of open source tools for the Control Center can be found here:

http://wiki.developspace.net/Open_Source_Engineering_Tools

Examples include a Java-based astrodynamics tool, tools for Mission Analysis, orbit determination and prediction, spacecraft simulation and modeling, a satellite constellation visualizer, a tool for solar sails, and more. As will be discussed later on in this book, a complete open source control center is available. This is the COSMOS product from Ball Aerospace. The author has direct hands-on experience implementing a cubesat control center, on a laptop, using this toolset.

Technology Readiness Levels

The Technology readiness level (TRL) is a measure of a facility's maturity for use. There are different TRL definitions by different agencies (NASA, DoD, ESA, FAA, DOE, etc). TRL are based on a scale from 1 to 9, with 9 being the most mature technology. The use of TRLs enables consistent, uniform, discussions of technical maturity across different types of technology. We will discuss the NASA one here, which was the original definition from the 1980's. It is generally applied to flight hardware, but can be used for the associated ground support infrastructure as well. TRL's can be applied to hardware or software, components, boxes, subsystems, or systems. Ultimately, we want the TRL level for the entire systems to be consistent with our flight requirements. Some components may have higher levels than needed. The TRL assessment allows us to consider the readiness and risk of our technology elements, and of the system.

Technology readiness levels in the National Aeronautics and Space Administration (NASA)

1. Basic principles observed and reported
This is the lowest "level" of technology maturation. At this level, scientific research begins to be translated into applied research and development.

2. Technology concept and/or application formulated
Once basic physical principles are observed, then at the next level of maturation, practical applications of those characteristics can be 'invented' or identified. At this level, the application is still speculative: there is not experimental proof or detailed analysis to support the conjecture.

3. Analytical and experimental critical function and/or characteristic proof of concept.

At this step in the maturation process, active research and

development (R&D) is initiated. This must include both analytical studies to set the technology into an appropriate context and laboratory-based studies to physically validate that the analytical predictions are correct. These studies and experiments should constitute "proof-of-concept" validation of the applications/concepts formulated at TRL 2.

4. Component and/or breadboard validation in laboratory environment.

Following successful "proof-of-concept" work, basic technological elements must be integrated to establish that the "pieces" will work together to achieve concept-enabling levels of performance for a component and/or breadboard. This validation must be devised to support the concept that was formulated earlier, and should also be consistent with the requirements of potential system applications. The validation is "low-fidelity" compared to the eventual system: it could be composed of ad hoc discrete components in a laboratory

TRL's can be applied to hardware or software, components, boxes, subsystems, or systems. Ultimately, we want the TRL level for the entire systems to be consistent with our flight requirements. Some components may have higher levels than needed.

5. Component and/or breadboard validation in relevant environment.

At this level, the fidelity of the component and/or breadboard being tested has to increase significantly. The basic technological elements must be integrated with reasonably realistic supporting elements so that the total applications (component-level, sub-system level, or system-level) can be tested in a 'simulated' or somewhat realistic environment.

6. System/subsystem model or prototype demonstration in a relevant environment (ground or space).

A major step in the level of fidelity of the technology demonstration follows the completion of TRL 5. At TRL 6, a representative model or prototype system or system - which would go well beyond ad hoc, 'patch-cord' or discrete component level breadboarding - would be tested in a relevant environment. At this level, if the only 'relevant environment' is the environment of space, then the model/prototype must be demonstrated in space.

7. System prototype demonstration in a space environment.

TRL 7 is a significant step beyond TRL 6, requiring an actual system prototype demonstration in a space environment. The prototype should be near or at the scale of the planned operational system and the demonstration must take place in space.

The TRL assessment allows us to consider the readiness and risk of our technology elements, and of the system.

Control Center as a Service

Do you need to own your own facility? Sometimes, yes. Many times, no. The main drivers for the Control Center implementation are mission safety and cost-effectiveness. A Cloud-based architecture can provide economies of scale, with security. After all, your credit card transactions are processed in the Cloud now. You can have whatever security you wish to pay for. You're not paying for hardware, software, or a bricks and mortar facility, but for a service. A Control Center is a central gathering place for multiple engineering disciplines to come together to support the mission. Can we virtualize this functionality, using "the cloud" and "the web"? Yes. But in times of crisis, when everything is going wrong, it is best to have every one in the same space, and allow direct interaction between staff. Just a dedicated room with tables, chairs, outlets, and wifi.

Using Control Center as a Service is particularly applicable to Constellations, as the solution and services scales in the Cloud architecture.

Virtualization

Virtualization provides a powerful tool for software development, testing, security, and operational environments. The Cloud architecture provides economy of scale in computing by shared resource usage. With virtualization, multiple "guest" operating systems can be run simultaneously under control of a "hypervisor." These guest operating systems do not need to all be the same. The Hypervisor manages the physical resources of the computer for the various guest operating systems, much as the operating systems do for the application code. The hardware resources include the central processing units, the various hierarchies of memory, and the input/output. Virtualization allows for server consolidation. It can ease migration and upgrade. Coupled with commodity computing, where you don't own the servers, but just rent time on them, a new economic model of hosting an operation like a satellite control center becomes easier.

We are talking her of virtualizing machines to support the Control Center Operation. There are two top level approaches to virtualization, the Process Virtual Machine, and the System Virtual machine. These two approaches differ in the implementation of the relationship of the Hypervisor and the operating system(s), with respect to the ring model of security.

A process virtual machine supports a single process. That single process provides a virtual model or abstraction of a certain machine model. Operating systems cannot operate in this environment unmodified, as they do not see the actual hardware. A good example is the Java Virtual Machine.

The Hypervisor is the operating system's operating system A hypervisor is a virtual machine manager. It manages virtual resources, including operating systems. It presents to a guest operating system a standard platform interface. Examples include XEN, VmWare, and QEMU. Hypervisors are top-level software supervisors that control the allocation of resources to multiple operating systems. Embedded hypervisors support real-time operations. The Hypervisor serves as a virtual machine manager. The Hypervisor runs on the host machine, and support one or more guest environments.

VmWare is a major commercial provider of proprietary virtualization and cloud solutions. Xen is a free and open source virtualization solution from the Computer Laboratory at the University of Cambridge, UK. There are many other virtualization solutions. As an aside, both Java and Android use a virtual machine approach.

Security in virtual systems can be a major concern. Some of the issues are addressed by existing protocols and standards for access and communications security. Security may also imply system stability and availability.

Cloud

Cloud Computing refers to a virtualized data center, accessible via high-bandwidth network connections. Its location is irrelevant to the applications. This allows the data center to be located in an area that is convenient to cheap electrical power, more secure, or where less cooling is required. Cloud computers provide utility computing services – units of computation on demand or on reserve. Administration of the data center and the virtual resources are centralized, and become port of the cost of services. This approach provides economy of scale to computer utilization. It allows company's to have large computing resources without the overhead of maintaining them. The computing or data services are delivered as services over a network.

Cloud Computing is economical because it allows sharing of the hardware resources without sharing the data. There's nothing magic going on. People who know what they're doing build, maintain, and manage the data center and its resources. If you're good at building satellites, not computing, you can buy computing as a service. This works because of the growth of high speed networks, mostly optical, driven by demand of the Internet.

Computing as a utility is the same concept as public utilities for water, electricity, gas, and, for that matter, the road network. These are resources that represent large capital investment, and provide services to multiple user's, who pay for their potion of use.

Amazon is widely regarded as being a major driver of the concept of Cloud Computing. They needed large amounts of hardware and data to manage their business. But, most of the time they had excess capacity for the average case, because of the need to address the maximum case. Amazon deployed the Cloud Model in their own datacenters, and rented out excess capacity. Amazon Web Services is a utility. At Acme Cubesats, where they are very good at what they do, their compute and data requirements are both platform and location independent. Amazon or a number of other facilities can rent them secure storage and as much compute time as they need when they need it. As with most commodities, the pricing model sets price by demand. At the end of the month, when every one does their accounting reports, computing is more expensive. Defer that by a week, and get better rates.

The Cloud model is scalable and elastic. It is easy to incorporate more hardware resources, and to power them down when they are not needed. They is enough spare hardware up and running to not only take care of peak demand, but to provide spares in case of failures. Virtual machines can be moved between compute platforms. A technique called load leveling monitors and optimizes the use of the hardware. This is the same process the electrical utilities use to determine that they have to bring additional generators online to meet peak air conditioning demand.

The National Institute of Standards and Technology issued a definition of Cloud Computing. This was authored by Peter Mell and Timothy Grance, and is NIST Special Publication 800-145 (September 2011). National Institute of Standards and Technology,

U.S. Department of Commerce. It is a short document, available for download. It says,

The five essential characteristics they define are:

"On-demand self-service. A consumer can unilaterally provision computing capabilities, such as server time and network storage, as needed automatically without requiring human interaction with each service provider.

Broad network access. Capabilities are available over the network and accessed through standard mechanisms that promote use by heterogeneous thin or thick client platforms (e.g., mobile phones, tablets, laptops, and workstations).

Resource pooling. The provider's computing resources are pooled to serve multiple consumers using a multi-tenant model, with different physical and virtual resources dynamically assigned and reassigned according to consumer demand.

Rapid elasticity. Capabilities can be elastically provisioned and released, in some cases automatically, to scale rapidly outward and inward commensurate with demand. To the consumer, the capabilities available for provisioning often appear to be unlimited and can be appropriated in any quantity at any time.

Measured service. Cloud systems automatically control and optimize resource use by leveraging a metering capability at some level of abstraction appropriate to the type of service (e.g., storage, processing, bandwidth, and active user accounts). Resource usage can be monitored, controlled, and reported, providing transparency for both the provider and consumer of the utilized service."

In addition, they list:

Service Models

Software as a Service (SaaS). The capability provided to the consumer is to use the provider's applications running on a cloud infrastructure2. The applications are accessible from various client devices through either a thin client interface, such as a web browser (e.g., web-based email), or a program interface. The consumer does not manage or control the underlying cloud infrastructure including network, servers, operating systems, storage, or even individual application capabilities, with the possible exception of limited user-specific application configuration settings.

Platform as a Service (PaaS). The capability provided to the consumer is to deploy onto the cloud infrastructure consumer-created or acquired applications created using programming languages, libraries, services, and tools supported by the provider.3 The consumer does not manage or control the underlying cloud infrastructure including network, servers, operating systems, or storage, but has control over the deployed applications and possibly configuration settings for the application-hosting environment.

Infrastructure as a Service (IaaS). The capability provided to the consumer is to provision processing, storage, networks, and other fundamental computing resources where the consumer is able to deploy and run arbitrary software, which can include operating systems and applications. The consumer does not manage or control the underlying cloud infrastructure but has control over operating systems, storage, and deployed applications; and possibly limited control of select networking components (e.g., host firewalls).

Deployment Models

Private cloud. The cloud infrastructure is provisioned for exclusive use by a single organization comprising multiple consumers (e.g., business units). It may be owned, managed, and operated by the organization, a third party, or some combination of them, and it

56

may exist on or off premises.

Community cloud. The cloud infrastructure is provisioned for exclusive use by a specific community of consumers from organizations that have shared concerns (e.g., mission, security requirements, policy, and compliance considerations). It may be owned, managed, and operated by one or more of the organizations in the community, a third party, or some combination of them, and it may exist on or off premises.

Public cloud. The cloud infrastructure is provisioned for open use by the general public. It may be owned, managed, and operated by a business, academic, or government organization, or some combination of them. It exists on the premises of the cloud provider.

Hybrid cloud. The cloud infrastructure is a composition of two or more distinct cloud infrastructures (private, community, or public) that remain unique entities, but are bound together by standardized or proprietary technology that enables data and application portability (e.g., cloud bursting for load balancing between clouds)."

You can access your Cubesat data in the cloud from a client as simple as a smartphone or tablet, no big desktop computer is required. At the same time, you can use these small appliances to log into your cloud-based virtual computer cluster, and control the running of programs with a simple application on your end. This is getting close to magic.

The technical aspects of Cloud Computing are simple and well understood. The implications and the business models are still evolving.

Security in the Cloud

There is naturally a concern about sending data and proprietary programs off somewhere nebulous. Cloud-based systems require new and innovative security measures. Cloud security is a barrier to adoption for many users, particularly satellite control centers. You are actually trusting some one else with a large part of your data and control security. One the other hand, a reputable provider will take this role very seriously, as even one incident can tarnish their reputation and lose them customers.

The issues of physical security for the cloud facility is well understood from previous architectures of large data centers and data repositories. The issue of secure data access can also be addressed, but this is a more serious concern. As with any system, absolute security cannot be achieved. Layered security and threat assessment provide levels of security for Cloud centers that are comparable to commercial and military standards for protection of physical and data resources.

A virtualized Satellite Control Center implements what is called "Control Center as a Service." Operators are not all seated in a large room of consoles, with a mainframe computer in the backroom. They are not necessarily all together in one room. They might be sitting at their desk, or accessing the data from their home computer, or on their phone at the coffee shop, maybe in their hot tub.

Where is the control center? In the Cloud! There is no big up-front cost in building the computational and communication resources. They are leased as needed.

This evolving service-oriented architecture (SOA) is an architectural pattern in computer software design in which application components provide services to other components via a communications protocol, typically over a network. The principles of service-orientation are independent of any vendor, product or technology. This has had wide application, and allows for implementing, upgrading, and improving services, without worrying about the basis technology.

We have come to believe that computation, data transmission, and data storage will continue to evolve according to a "Moore's law" (exponential growth curve). That has been the case since the development of solid state, semiconductor materials. It is not a sustainable long term model, but it has worked well so far. It allows develops (of spacecraft support systems) to focus on what needs done, rather than on how to do it. It allows for technology refresh easily. It drives the economy in terms of new paradigms (like satellite TV and Internet ordering of goods and services). It does produce sometimes a realization that you may not actually know where activities and data are. In one sense, you don't care. They're in the cloud. However, due-diligence with important and costly assets is called for. Companies have evolved that mastered the new paradigms, and are expert at the new way of doing things.

Fly the Control Center

In Constellation missions, particularly for those not in Earth Orbit, a local control center/first responder would be valuable. We will talk of this in the context of asteroid mission for Cubesats.

The mission will consist of a large "mothership" to transport and deploy the Cubesats. In this concept, the Cubesats are the primary payload. The Mothership can be thought of as a very large Cubesat. The architecture is kept as close as possible.

Use of a common hardware bus and software architecture for all swarm members, to the greatest extent possible, is a goal. Only the sensor sets will be unique. A Cubesat model for the hardware, and NASA GSFC's Core Flight Software is baselined. A standard linux software operating environment and database will be used. In addition, the Mothership will implement the COSMOS product, actually, multiple instances, as discussed in the Control Center as a Cloud discussion.

Use of a common hardware bus and software architecture for all swarm members, to the greatest extent possible, is a goal. Only the sensor sets will be unique. A Cubesat model for the hardware, and NASA GSFC's Core Flight Software is baselined. A standard linux software operating environment and database will be used.

Using standard linux clustering software (Beowulf), the Mothership and undeployed swarm members will be able to form an ad-hoc cluster computer to process science data in-situ. This can be implement with hard-wired network connections. For deployed Cubesats to participate requires new data transmission protocols, and a re-look at transceivers for the units. The explorer Cubesats can be dispatched to targets of convenience, and co-operate by doing simultaneous observations

LAN-based Mesh network software will be used. The Mothership's main computer will be a Raspberry-Pi based cluster. The mothership maintains a large data repository for those times when the link to Earth is not available (due to opposition), and also has a large, perhaps laser-based, communications link to Earth. It's job is to aggregate the data send back, and optimize the link for speed and accuracy.

By using the same control center software on the Mothership and the ground-based control center, we gain equivalent architectures and formats. The onboard version can be augmented with a Virtual operator, an AI for making on-site decisions in response to local events. None of this is beyond the capability of a 64-node Rasbperry-Pi based Beowulf Cluster, with watchdogs using Rad-Hard Pi technology.

GMSEC

GMSEC is the Goddard Mission Services Evolution Center, developed and maintained by the Software Engineering Division, Ground Software Systems Branch of NASA/GFSC (Code 583). It is the go-to starting point for Goddard mission control centers. It was established in 2001 to bring together best practices and best architectures of ground and flight data systems. It functions to standardize interfaces, and to develop and maintain a middleware interface for control center developers. With the interface, most COTS hardware and software solutions can be used. GMSEC bridges the gap between mission-specific components and services, and a large set of general hardware and software solutions. It is an evolvable solution, with, at this writing, nearly 15 years of experience with real missions.

The GMSEC API defines the interface between applications and the GMSEC middleware. Standardized messaging and the support of numerous languages comes with the package. It also supports a variety of open source and proprietary operating systems.

The GEMSEC System Agent is used to communicate health information about the host (s). It can be used to monitor resources such as memory and cpu loading.

GMSEC includes the Criteria Action Tool, which collects data, analyzes it, and makes decisions based on rules and policies regarding corrective actions. It is a monitor-only function, and is working in the background to assist in monitoring the ground system.

The Room Alert Adapter uses the AVTECH Room Alert system to monitor the environment of the physical Control Center, in the areas of temperature, humidity, power status, and flooding. It can implement rule-based automated corrective action. This would be of particular value to a remote, unmanned facility.

GMSEC also has the ability to send selected messages to a web server for dissemination, with the proper encryption.

https://gmsec.gsfc.nasa.gov/

ITOS

ITOS, The Integrated Test and Operations System, is a real-time control and monitoring system which works with the GMSEC concept. It is hosted on Unix (including linux). It provides the functionality of an Integration and Test environment, a spacecraft control center, or applies to any control and monitoring system. It is built around a database, and includes a web interface. It can work well in a light-out environment. It provides a variety of functions for remote monitoring and control of a complex system, and has a flexible display architecture. It includes a STOL language. It can interface with a long list of ground stations, and the Internet.

Another product maintained by the Ground Software Systems Branch of GSFC is ASIST (Advanced Spacecraft Integration and System Test. This product is workstation-based and scalable. It uses standard network and operating system components. It supports CCSDS protocols for telemetry and command. It supports mass storage, scalable for an entire mission's history. It also has built-in rule-based monitoring.

SOI – a University Satellite Control Center

SOI – the Systems Operations Institute at Capitol Technical University in Laurel, Maryland, is a full-up satellite command and control center, linked to nearby NASA-Goddard Space Flight Center by a high-speed data line. It was established in 2002 with a NASA grant, and operates as NASA/Industry/Education partnership. It provides training in satellite operations to students who can then go on to Internships and full time employment at NASA. It can also serve as a backup/fallback control facility. It has supported six orbiting satellite projects to date. According to Capitol, "Satellites operated by students at SOI are either in extended mode operations or pre-launch preparation. Extended mode missions have already met their primary objectives by NASA's terms, but are still healthy and capable of producing valuable scientific data. By allowing students to utilize "expired" satellites as learning tools, NASA saves millions of dollars by keeping projects going longer than anticipated, while training the next generation of flight controllers and system engineers." The SOI is based on commercial pc architectures, and has a dozen stations running Windows-7, and linux.

A Cubesat Control Center

During the summers of 2015 and 2016, the author taught courses in Cubesat Engineering, and Operations at Capitol Technology University in Laurel, Maryland.

The SOI was used to host the Cubesat facility. In the adjacent room, the students built their Cubesat prototypes, not-for-flight, using a Raspberry Pi as the onboard computer. The Pi included software modules from NASA/GSFC's Open Source cFS (core Flight System), and custom scripts written in the Python and C languages.

The control center software COSMOS, from Ball Aerospace, was hosted on a standard laptop machine. Since COSMOS is open source, it was modified slightly to provide telemetry data from the cubesat directly to the Apache web server, running on the same host machine. The Telemetry data, once posted on the website, could be accessed by other computers over the web, and by tablets and smart phones. The following picture shows the various COSMOS applications provided.

A screenshot form COSMOS is shown on the next page.

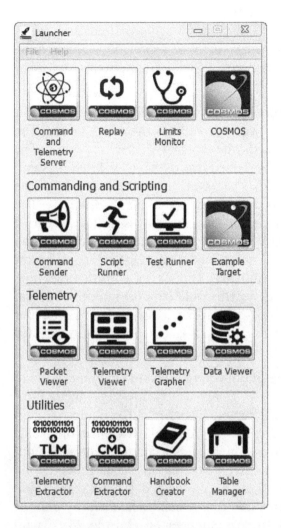

Courtesy, Ball Aerospace

The modularity and open design of COSMOS greatly enabled the project. COSMOS includes 15 modules to send commands; receive, archive, and visualize data; monitor red and yellow limits; and can support automated procedures. It is available for download as an open source product, and runs on Windows and Linux.

At the beginning, we decided that the desired solution would be totally open source. This was implemented using the COSMOS software under Ubuntu Linux. The Apache webserver was added. Using features of the COSMOS system, formatted and limit-checked telemetry were passed to the web server. This allowed the end user terminal to be laptops, tablets, smartphones, or other personal devices.

COSMOS can support more than active satellite missions. In our case, the engineering lab was located in the next room. The Cubesats communicated with the control center via wifi. The flatsats in the lab could be tested from the COSMOS system. Supporting both test and operations allowed for a single architecture that was co-developed with the hardware. The advantage of this approach is that there was not a separate Integration & Test support system and Operations System. When Integration and Test was completed, the Operations Support Software was ready, and validated. This saves considerable time and money. In addition, the system could support multiple cubesat "targets" simultaneously on the same machine. The number depends solely on bandwidth, memory, and computation cycles available. The solution is scalable, and can be virtualized.

In terms of a lights-out operation, where relevant personnel receive converted data via web access, email, or text message, the control center function has been abstracted. There is still a control center, but you don't need to be there to do your job. It can be operated-lights out. A key item to consider is inter-team communication, provided by various corroborative meeting aps. This removes the requirement that team members be co-located. At the same time, routine monitoring of events and trends can be handled by control center software, a virtual system engineer on console 24x7, who doesn't need to sleep or go to the bathroom. This agent software can learn the characteristics of the system, as it ages. We hesitate to use the term artificial intelligence here, but...

Telemetry received by COSMOS is logged as binary, and goes through the Telemetry Extractor process, which produces a text file. It can then be viewed as packets, as extracted telemetry, Engineering units, or graphed. There is also a limit checking process that can be set up on selected telemetry. This involves defining yellow and red limits for each telemetry point.

The link between COSMOS and Apache was implemented by taking the Telemetry Extractor's file and converting it from text to HTML format. This new files were accessible to the Apache web server. The data was put up on the local web, and could be viewed remotely.

COSMOS is implemented in Ruby, an open source, object-oriented language. COSMOS refers to the system it is communicating with as the "target." Thus, we defined the command and telemetry files for the target "Pi." We could support multiple targets with unique identifiers, but this feature was not implemented due to time constraints.

Automation was used to reduce the manual workload. Routine operations can be handled by the systems itself, with oversight. Automated detection and response to anomalies can be phased in. A wide range of situational awareness tools with visibility across subsystems can be implemented and verified.

Consider the alert system. The easiest implementation is a simple, predefined red-limits, yellow-limits monitoring. As time progresses, the hardware ages, and the limits need to be adjusted. At the same time, the limits monitor can learn and become smarter, both about pre-set limits, but also about the interaction of multiple sampling points. Alerts can be distributed by pop-up boxes on screens, or test message.

The system is being considered to support Capitol's 2018 Cubesat mission. Further additions will include a secure remote commanding capability, limits-violations text messages, and a "smart" limits checker, that acts as a virtual system engineer on console, deciding when human intervention is needed. This automation of routine tasks allows the control center staff to focus on the exceptions. About the only feature not needed is propulsion support, as Cubesats by definition have no propulsion system.

NASA /GSFC is looking into using this approach for their own Cubesat projects.

Other off-the shelf Control Center software packages include NASA/GSFC's ITOS and Epoch2000 from Kratos Integral Systems. These may be overkill for most Cubesat missions.

COSMOS works hand-in-had with Goddard's Core Flight Software. This is a set of routines that run under an operating system on the cubesat. Everything is almost plug-and-play.

The Core Flight Executive, from the Flight Software Branch at NASA/GSFC, is an open source operating system framework. The executive is a set of mission independent reusable software services and an operating environment. Within this architecture, various mission-specific applications can be hosted. The cFE focuses on the commonality of flight software. The Core Flight System (CFS) supplies libraries and applications. Much flight software legacy went into the concept of the cFE. It has gotten traction within the NASA community, and is in use on many flight projects, simulators, and test beds (FlatSats) at multiple NASA centers, as well as functioning in on-orbit Cubesats.

The Galaxy command and telemetry system is a commercial follow-on to ITOS, developed by the Hammers Company. It is compliant with the CCSDS standards, and is database-centric. It can also function as a spacecraft simulator. It is compatible with NASA/GSFC's cFE/CFS flight (onboard) software. STARS is another Hammers product for command and telemetry that can be web-based, and can provide web-based access. It is also multi-mission capable.

Epoch2000

The Epoch 2000 software package is a proprietary product of Integral Systems, now Kratos/ISI. It is currently in its fourth version. It provides command and control functions for a satellite, or constellation of satellites. Epoch is hosted on Microsoft Windows. It is built on CORBA (Common Object Brokered Architecture). It includes an offline telemetry analysis and display tool known as ABE – the Archive Browser and Extractor. Epoch Client supplies a data visualization and analysis tool with plotting capability. Epoch is built around an Oracle database. The orbit analysis system within Epoch is called OASYS.

Kratos also offers the quantum command and control package (quantumCMD), a lightweight system intended for small satellites. QuantumCMD also implements a web interface. It is designed to handle between 1500 and 2000 telemetry points, hosted on a single server. It is hosted on Linux.

GENSO

The Global Educational Network for Satellite Operations (Genso) is a software standard, started at ESA, with a series of ground stations around the world. It was developed for Cubesats. It was started in 2007.

Genso has a ground station server and a mission control client in the software architecture. Additionally, there is an Authentication Server, to restrict access to registered satellites, and authorized users. The Amateur Radio Community, worldwide, provides the Radio Frequency (RF) equipment and services. Ground stations operate 24x7. The Genso software is written in Java.

Ref:
http://m.esa.int/Education/Global_Educational_Network_for_Satellite_Operations

Wrap-up

The satellite control center has evolved greatly since it's use in the 1950's, and its basis hardware and software has improved by many orders of magnitude. But, its mission remains the same: command and control of the satellite, monitor its performance, and collect the data it sends. We have more and better tools to do this. Control Center architecture will continue to evolve in the future.

Whether we are supporting a single Cubesat mission in Earth orbit, or a constellation of Cubesats heading to Jupiter, the approach is the same – it is only a matter of scale. Most of the pieces exist.

Glossary

1553 – Military standard data bus, serial, 1 Mbps.

1U – one unit for a Cubesat, 10 x 10 x 10 cm.

3U – three units for a Cubesat

6u – 6 units in size, where 1u is defined by dimensions and weight.

802.11 – a radio frequency wireless data communications standard.

AACS – (JPL) Attitude and articulation control system.

ACE – attitude control electronics

Actuator – device which converts a control signal to a mechanical action.

Ada – a computer language.

A/D, ADC – analog to digital converter

AFB – Air Force Base.

AFSCN – (U. S.) Air Force Satellite Control Network.

AGC – Automated guidance and control.

AIAA – American Institute of Aeronautics and Astronautics.

AIST – NASA GSFC Advanced Information System Technology .

ALU – arithmetic logic unit.

AmSat – Amateur Satellite. Favored by Ham Radio operators as communication relays.

Analog – concerned with continuous values.

ANSI – American National Standards Institute

Android – an operating system based on Gnu-Linux, popular for smart phones and tablet computers.

Antares – Space launch vehicle, compatible with Cubesats, by Orbital/ATK (U.S.)

AP – application programs.

API – application program interface; specification for software modules to communicate.

APL – Applied Physics Laboratory, of the Johns Hopkins University.

APM – antenna pointing mechanism

Apollo – US manned lunar program.

ARC – (NASA) Ames Research Center

Arduino – a small, inexpensive microcontroller architecture.

Arinc – Aeronautical Radio, Inc. commercial company supporting transportation, and providing standards for avionics.

ARM – Acorn RISC machine; a 32-bit architecture with wide application in embedded systems.

ARPA – (U. S.) Advanced Research Projects Agency.

ArpaNet – Advanced Research Projects Agency (U.S.), first packet switched network, 1968.

ASIC – application specific integrated circuit

async – non synchronized

ATAC – Applied Technologies Advanced Computer.

ATP – authority to proceed

AU – astronomical unit. Roughly 93 million miles, the mean distance between Earth and Sun,

BAE – British Aerospace.

Baud – symbol rate; may or may not be the same as bit rate.

BCD – binary coded decimal. 4-bit entity used to represent 10 different decimal digits; with 6 spare states.

Beowolf – a cluster of commodity computers; multiprocessor, using Linux.

Big-endian – data format with the most significant bit or byte at the lowest address, or transmitted first.

Binary – using base 2 arithmetic for number representation.

BIST – built-in self test.

Bit – binary variable, value of 1 or 0.

Boolean – a data type with two values; an operation on these data types; named after George Boole, mid-19th century inventor of Boolean algebra.

Bootloader – initial program run after power-on or reset. Gets the computer up & going.

Bootstrap – a startup or reset process that proceeds without external intervention.

BSD – Berkeley Software Distribution version of the Bell Labs Unix operating system.

BP - bundle protocol, for dealing with errors and disconnects.

BSP – board support package. Customization Software and device drivers.

Buffer – a temporary holding location for data.

Bug – an error in a program or device.

Bus – an electrical connection between 2 or more units; the engineering part of the spacecraft.

byte – a collection of 8 bits

C – programming language from Bell Labs, circa 1972.

cache – temporary storage between cpu and main memory.

Cache coherency – process to keep the contents of multiple caches consistent,

CalPoly – California Polytechnic State University,. San Luis Obispo, CA.

CAN - controller area network bus.

CCSDS – Consultive Committee on Space Data Systems.

CDR – critical design review

C&DH – Command and Data Handling

CDFP - CCSDS File Delivery Protocol

cFE – Core Flight Executive – NASA GSFC reusable flight software.

CFS – Core Flight System – NASA GSFC reusable flight software.

Chip – integrated circuit component.

Clock – periodic timing signal to control and synchronize operations.

CME – Coronal Mass Ejection. Solar storm.

CMOS – complementary metal oxide semiconductor; a technology using both positive and negative semiconductors to achieve low power operation.

CogE – cognizant engineer for a particular discipline; go-to guy; specialist.

Complement – in binary logic, the opposite state.

Compilation – software process to translate source code to assembly or machine code (or error codes).

Configware – equivalent of software for FPGA architectures; configuration information.

Constellation – a grouping of satellites.

Control Flow – computer architecture involving directed flow through the program; data dependent paths are allowed.

COP – computer operating properly.

Coprocessor – another processor to supplement the operations of the main processor. Used for floating point, video, etc. Usually relies on the main processor for instruction fetch; and control.

Cordic – Coordinate Rotation Digital Computer – to calculate hyberbolic and trig functions.

Cots – commercial, off the shelf

CPU – central processing unit

D/A – digital to analog conversion.

DAC – digital to analog converter.

Daemon – in multitasking, a program that runs in the background.

DARPA – Defense advanced research projects agency.

Dataflow – computer architecture where a changing value forces recalculation of dependent values.

Datagram – message on a packet switched network; the delivery, arrival time, and order of arrival are not guaranteed.

dc – direct current.

D-cache – data cache.

DDR – dual data rate memory.

Deadlock – a situation in which two or more competing actions are each waiting for the other to finish, and thus neither ever does.

DCE – data communications equipment; interface to the network.

Deadly embrace – a deadlock situation in which 2 processes are each waiting for the other to finish.

Denorm – in floating point representation, a non-zero number with a magnitude less than the smallest normal number.

Device driver – specific software to interface a peripheral to the operating system.

Digital – using discrete values for representation of states or numbers.

Dirty bit – used to signal that the contents of a cache have changed.

Discrete – single bit signal.

DMA – direct memory access.

Dnepr – Russian space launch system compatible with Cubesats.

DOD – (U. S.) Department of Defense.

74

DOE – (U. S.) Department of Energy.

DOF – degrees of freedom.

Downlink – from space to earth.

Dram – dynamic random access memory.

DSP – digital signal processing/processor.

DTE – data terminal equipment; communicates with the DCE to get to the network.

DTN – delay tolerant networks.

DUT – device under test.

ECC – error correcting code

EDAC – error detecting and correction circuitry.

EDAC – error detection and correction.

EGSE – electrical ground support equipment

EIA – Electronics Industry Association.

ELV – expendable launch vehicle.

Embedded system – a computer systems with limited human interfaces and performing specific tasks. Usually part of a larger system.

EMC – electromagnetic compatibility.

EMI – electromagnetic interference.

EOL – end of life.

EOS – Earth Observation spacecraft.

Ephemeris – orbital position data.

Epitaxial – in semiconductors, have a crystalline overlayer with a well-defined orientation.

EPS – electrical power subsystem.

ESA – European Space Organization.

ESRO – European Space Research Organization

ESTO – NASA/GSFC – Earth Science Technology Office.

Ethernet – networking protocol, IEEE 802.3

ev – electron volt, unit of energy

EVA – extra-vehicular activity.

Exception – interrupt due to internal events, such as overflow.

EXPRESS racks – on the ISS, EXpedite the PRocessing of Experiments for Space Station Racks

FAA – (U S.) Federal Aviation Administration.

Fail-safe – a system designed to do no harm in the event of failure.

Falcon – launch vehicle from SpaceX.

FCC – (U.S.) Federal Communications Commission.

FDC – fault detection and correction.

Firewire – IEEE-1394 standard for serial communication.

Firmware – code contained in a non-volatile memory.

Fixed point – computer numeric format with a fixed number of digits or bits, and a fixed radix point. Integers.

Flag – a binary state variable.

Flash – non-volatile memory

Flatsat – prototyping and test setup, laid out on a bench for easy access.

FlightLinux – NASA Research Program for Open Source code in space.

Floating point – computer numeric format for real numbers; has significant digits and an exponent.

FPGA – field programmable gate array.

FPU – floating point unit, an ALU for floating point numbers.

Full duplex – communication in both directions simultaneously.

Fram – ferromagnetic RAM; a non-volatile memory technology

FRR – Flight Readiness Review

FSW – flight software.

FTP – file transfer protocol

Gbyte – 10^9 bytes.

GEO – geosynchronous orbit.

GeV – billion (109) electron volts.

GNC – guidance, navigation, and control.

Gnu – recursive acronym, gnu is not unix.

GPIO – general purpose I/O.

GPL – gnu public license used for free software; referred to as the "copyleft."

GPS – Global Positioning system – Navigation satellites.

GPU – graphics processing unit. ALU for graphics data.

GSFC – Goddard Space Flight Center, Greenbelt, MD.

Gyro – (gyroscope) a sensor to measure rotation.

Half-duplex – communications in two directions, but not simultaneously.

HAL/S – computer language.

Handshake – co-ordination mechanism.

HDL – hardware description language

Hertz – cycles per second.

Hexadecimal – base 16 number representation.

Hi-rel – high reliability

HPCC – High Performance Computing and Communications.

Hypervisor – virtual machine manager. Can manage multiple operating systems.

I2C – a serial communications protocol.

IARU – International Amateur Radio Union

I-cache – Instruction cache.

ICD – interface control document.

IC&DH – Instrument Command & Data Handling.

IEEE – Institute of Electrical and Electronic engineers

IEEE-754 – standard for floating point representation and calculation.

IIC – inter-integrated circuit (I/O).

IMU – inertial measurement unit.

Integer – the natural numbers, zero, and the negatives of the natural numbers.

Interrupt – an asynchronous event to signal a need for attention (example: the phone rings).

Interrupt vector – entry in a table pointing to an interrupt service routine; indexed by interrupt number.

IP – intellectual property; Internet protocol.

IP core – IP describing a chip design that can be licensed to be used in an FPGA or ASIC.

IP-in-Space – Internet Protocol in Space.

IR – infrared, 1-400 terahertz. Perceived as heat.

IRAD – Independent Research & Development.

ISA – instruction set architecture, the software description of the computer.

ISO – International Standards Organization.

ISR – interrupt service routine, a subroutine that handles a particular interrupt event.

ISS – International Space Station

I&T – integration & test

ITAR – International Trafficking in Arms Regulations (U.S. Dept. of   State)

ITU – International Telecommunications Union

IV&V – Independent validation and verification.

JEM – Japanese Experiment Module, on the ISS.

JHU – Johns Hopkins University.

JPL – Jet Propulsion Laboratory

JSC – Johnson Space Center, Houston, Texas.

JTAG – Joint Test Action Group; industry group that lead to IEEE 1149.1, Standard Test Access Port and Boundary-Scan Architecture.

JWST – James Webb Space Telescope – follow on to Hubble.

Kbps – kilo (10^3) bits per second.

Kernel – main portion of the operating system. Interface between the applications and the hardware.

Kg – kilogram.

kHz – kilo (10^3) hertz

KVA – kilo volts amps – a measure of electrical power

Ku band – 12-18 Ghz radio

Lan – local area network, wired or wireless

LaRC – (NASA) Langley Research Center.

Latchup – condition in which a semiconductor device is stuck in one state.

Lbf – pounds-force.

LEO – low Earth orbit.

Let- Linear Energy Transfer

Lidar – optical radar.

Linux – open source operating system.

List – a data structure.

Little-endian – data format with the least significant bit or byte at the highest address, or transmitted last.

Logic operation – generally, negate, AND, OR, XOR, and their inverses.

Loop-unrolling – optimization of a loop for speed at the cost of space.

LRU – least recently used; an algorithm for item replacement in a cache.

LSB – least significant bit or byte.

LSP – (NASA) launch services program, or launch services provider

LUT – look up table.

Master-slave – control process with one element in charge. Master status may be exchanged among elements.

Mbps – mega (10^6) bits per second.

Mbyte – one million (10^6 or 2^{20}) bytes.

Memory leak – when a program uses memory resources but does not return them, leading to a lack of available memory.

MEMS – Micro Electronic Mechanical System.

MESI – modified, exclusive, shared, invalid state of a cache coherency protocol.

MEV – million electron volts.

MHz – one million (10^6) Hertz

Microcontroller – monolithic cpu + memory + I/O.

Microkernel – operating system which is not monolithic, functions execute in user space.

Microprocessor – monolithic cpu.

Microsat – satellite with a mass between 10 and 100 kg.

Microsecond – 10^{-6} second.

Microkernel – operating system which is not monolithic. So functions execute in user space.

MLI – multi-layer insulation.

MPA – multiple payload adapter for deploying multiple p-pod's

MPE – Maximum predicted environments.

mram – magnetorestrictive random access memory.

mSec – Millisecond; (10-3) second.

MIPS – millions of instructions per second.

MMU – memory management unit; manned maneuvering unit.

MSB – most significant bit or byte.

Multiplex – combining signals on a communication channel by sampling.

Multicore – multiple processing cores on one substrate or chip; need not be identical.

Mutex – a software mechanism to provide mutual exclusion between tasks.

Nano – 10^{-9}

NanoRacks – a company providing a facility onboard the ISS to support Cubesats.

nanoSat – small satellite with a mass between 1 and 10 kg.

NASA - National Aeronautics and Space Administration.

NDA – non-disclosure agreement; legal agreement protecting IP.

NEN – (NASA's) Near Earth Network

Nibble – 4 bits, ½ byte.

NIST – National Institute of Standards and Technology (US), previously, National Bureau of Standards.

NMI – non-maskable interrupt; cannot be ignored by the software.

Normalized number – in the proper format for floating point representation.

NRCSD - NanoRack CubeSat Deployer

NRE – non-recurring engineering; one-time costs for a project.

NSF – (U.S.) National Science Foundation.

NSR – non-space rated.

NTIA (U.S.) National Telecommunications and Information Administration

NUMA – non-uniform memory access for multiprocessors; local and global memory access protocol.

NVM – non-volatile memory.

NWS – (U.S.) National Weather Service

Nyquist rate – in communications, the minimum sampling rate, equal to twice the highest frequency in the signal.

OBC – on board computer

OBD – On-Board diagnostics.

OBP – On Board Processor

Off-the-shelf – commercially available; not custom.

OpAmp – (Linear) operational amplifier; linear gain and isolation stage.

OpCode – encoded computer instruction.

Open source – methodology for hardware or software development with free distribution and access.

Operating system – software that controls the allocation of

resources in a computer.

OSAL – operating system abstraction layer.

OSI – Open systems interconnect model for networking, from ISO.

Overflow - the result of an arithmetic operation exceeds the capacity of the destination.

Packet – a small container; a block of data on a network.

Paging – memory management technique using fixed size memory blocks.

Paradigm – a pattern or model

Paradigm shift – a change from one paradigm to another. disruptive or evolutionary.

Parallel – multiple operations or communication proceeding simultaneously.

Parity – an error detecting mechanism involving an extra check bit in the word.

Pc – personal computer.

PC-104 – standard for a board (90 x 96 mm), and a bus for embedded use.

PCB – printed circuit board.

pci – personal computer interface (bus).

PCM – pulse code modulation.

PDR – preliminary design review

Peta - 10^{15} or 2^{50}

Phonesat – small satellite using a cell phone for onboard control and computation.

Picosat – small satellite with a mass between 0.1 and 1 kg.

Piezo – production of electricity by mechanical stress.

Pinout – mapping of signals to I/O pins of a device.

Pipeline – operations in serial, assembly-line fashion.

PiSat – a Cubesat architecture developed at NASA-GSFC, based on the Raspberry Pi architecture.

Pixel – picture element; smallest addressable element on a display or a sensor.

PLL – phase locked loop.

PocketQube – smaller than a Cubesat; 5 cm cubed, a mass of no more than 180 grams, and uses COTS components.

Poc – point of contact

POSIX – IEEE standard operating system.

PPF – payload processing facility

PPL – preferred parts list (NASA).

P-POD – Cubesat launch dispenser, Poly-Picosatellite Orbital Deployer

Psia – pounds per square inch, absolute.

PSP – Platform Support Package.

PWM – pulse width modulation.

Python – programming language.

Quadrature encoder – an incremental rotary encoder providing rotational position information.

Queue – first in, first out data buffer structure; implemented in hardware or software.

Rad – unit of radiation exposure

Rad750 – A radiation hardened IBM PowerPC cpu.

Radix point – separates integer and fractional parts of a real number.

RAID – redundant array of inexpensive disks.

Ram – random access memory.

RBF – remove before flight.

Real-time – system that responds to events in a predictable, bounded time.

Register – temporary storage location for a data item.

Reset – signal and process that returns the hardware to a known, defined state.

RF – radio frequency

RFC – request for comment

RISC – reduced instruction set computer.

RHPPC – Rad-Hard Power PC.

RISC – reduced instruction set computer.

Router – networking component for packets.

RS-232/422/423 – asynchronous and synchronous serial communication standards.

RT – remote terminal.

RTC – real time clock.

RTOS – real time operating system.

SAM – sequential access memory, like a magnetic tape.

Sandbox – an isolated and controlled environment to run untested or potentially malicious code.

SDR – software defined radio

SDRAM – synchronous dynamic random access memory.

Segmentation – dividing a network or memory into sections.

Semiconductor – material with electrical characteristics between conductors and insulators; basis of current technology processor, memory, and I/O devices, as well as sensors.

Semaphore – a binary signaling element among processes.

SD – secure digital (non-volatile memory card).

SDVF – Software Development and Validation Facility.

Sensor – a device that converts a physical observable quantity or event to a signal.

Serial – bit by bit.

SEU – single event upset (radiation induced error).

Servo – a control device with feedback.

SIMD – single instruction, multiple data (parallel processing)

Six-pack – a six U Cubesat, 10 x 20 x 30 cm.

SMP – symmetric multiprocessing.

Snoop – monitor packets in a network, or data in a cache.

SN – (NASA's) Space Network

SOA – safe operating area; also, state of the art.

SOCC – spacecraft operations control center

Socket – an end-point in communication across a network

Soft core – a hardware description language description of a cpu core.

Software – set of instructions and data to tell a computer what to do.

SMP – symmetric multiprocessing.

Snoop – monitor packets in a network, or data in a cache.

Spacewire – high speed (160 Mbps) link.

SPI - Serial Peripheral Interface - a synchronous serial communication interface.

SRAM – static random access memory.

Stack – first in, last out data structure. Can be hardware or software.

Stack pointer – a reference pointer to the top of the stack.

STAR – self test and repair.

State machine – model of sequential processes.

STOL – system test oriented language, a scripting language for testing systems.

T&I – test and integration.

Terrabyte – 10^{12} bytes.

SAA – South Atlantic anomaly. High radiation zone.

SEB – single event burnout.

SEU – single event upset.

SEL – single event latchup.

Soc – state of charge; system on a chip.

Soft core – hardware description description language model of a logic core.

SOI – silicon on insulator

SoS – silicon on sapphire – an inherently radiation-hard technology

spi – serial peripheral interface

SpaceCube – an advanced FPGA-based flight computer.

SpaceWire – networking and interconnect standard.

Space-X – commercial space company.

SRAM – static random access memory.

Stack – first in, last out data structure. Can be hardware or software.

Stack pointer – a reference pointer to the top of the stack.

State machine – model of sequential processes.

SWD – serial wire debug.

Synchronous – using the same clock to coordinate operations.

System – a collection of interacting elements and relationships with a specific behavior.

System of Systems – a complex collection of systems with pooled resources.

Suitsat – old Russian spacesuit, instrumented with an 8-bit micro, and launched from the ISS.

Swarm – a collection of satellites that can operate cooperatively.

sync – synchronize, synchronized.

TCP/IP – Transmission Control Protocol/Internet protocol.

TDRSS – Tracking and Data Relay satellite system.

Tera - 10^{12} or 2^{40}

Test-and-set – coordination mechanism for multiple processes that allows reading to a location and writing it in a non-interruptible manner.

TCP/IP – transmission control protocol/internet protocol; layered set of protocols for networks.

Thread – smallest independent set of instructions managed by a multiprocessing operating system.

TID – total ionizing dose.

TMR – triple modular redundancy.

Toolchain – set of software tools for development.

Transceiver – receiver and transmitter in one box.

Transducer – a device that converts one form of energy to another.

Train – a series of satellites in the same or similar orbits, providing sequential observations.

TRAP – exception or fault handling mechanism in a computer; an operating system component.

Triplicate – using three copies (of hardware, software, messaging, power supplies, etc.). for redundancy and error control.

TRL – technology readiness level

Truncate – discard. cutoff, make shorter.

TT&C – tracking, telemetry, and command.

ttl – transistor-transistor logic integrated circuit.

UART – Universal asynchronous receiver-transmitter.

UDP – User datagram protocol; part of the Internet Protocol.

uM – micro (10^{-6}) meter

Underflow – the result of an arithmetic operation is smaller than the smallest representable number.

UoSat – a family of small spacecraft from Surrey Space Technology Ltd. (UK).

Uplink – from ground to space.

USB – universal serial bus.

VDC – volts, direct current.

Vector – single dimensional array of values.

VHDL – very high level design language.

VIA – vertical conducting pathway through an insulating layer.

Virtual memory – memory management technique using address translation.

Virtualization – creating a virtual resource from available physical resources.

Virus – malignant computer program.

Viterbi Decoder – a maximum likelihood decoder for data encoded with a Convolutional code for error control. Can be implemented in software or hardware

VLIW – very long instruction word – mechanism for parallelism.

VxWorks – real time operating system from Wind River systems.

WiFi – short range digital radio.

Watchdog – hardware/software function to sanity check the hardware, software, and process; applies corrective action if a fault is detected; fail-safe mechanism.

Wiki – the Hawaiian word for "quick." Refers to a collaborative content website.

Word – a collection of bits of any size; does not have to be a power of two.

Write-back – cache organization where the data is not written to main memory until the cache location is needed for re-use.

Write-through – all cache writes also go to main memory.

X-band – 7 – 11 GHz.

Xilinx – manufacturer of programmable logic and FPGA's.

Yagi – a directional antenna with multiple half-wave dipole rods.

Zener – voltage reference diode.

Zero address – architecture using implicit addressing, like a stack.

Zombie-sat – a dead satellite, in orbit.

ZOE - Zone of Exclusion, volume in which the presence of an object or personnel, or activities are prohibited

References

CCSDS, *Report concerning Space Data Systems Standards, Mission Operations Services concept*, Green Book, CCSDS 520.0 December 2010.

Cudmore, Alan *NASA/GSFC's Flight Software Architecture: core Flight Executive and Core Flight System*, NASA/GSFC Code 582.

Johnson, Michael Peter, *Mission Control: Inventing the Groundwork of Spaceflight,* 2015, University Press of Florida, ISBN- 0813061504.

Kraft, Christopher, *Flight: My Life in Mission Control*, 2001, Dutton Adult, ISBN-0525945717

Kraft, Christopher, *Failure is Not an Option: Mission Control from Mercury to Apollo 13 and Beyond*, 2009, Simon & Schuster.

De Jardins, Richard, *Payload Operations Control Center Network (POCCNET) Systems Definition Phase*, January 1978, NASDA-TM-79567.

Elbert, Bruce R. *Introduction to Satellite Communication*, 2nd ed, Artech House Publishers, 1998. ISBN-10: 0890069611.

Galal, Ken *Satellite Mission Operations Best Practices, Flight Dynamics,* 2001, NASA Ames Research Center.1.

Griffith, Robert C. *Mobile CubeSat Command and Control (MC3)*, Feb. 2012, Amazon Digital Services, ASIN B007B4LWBBO.

Harvey, Ray, *Satellite Mission Operations Best Practices,* April 18, 2003, BEST PRACTICES WORKING GROUP, SPACE OPERATIONS AND SUPPORT TECHNICAL COMMITTEE, AIAA

Howard, Joseph, Oza, Dipak *Best Practices for Operations of Satellite Constellations*,
ntrs.nasa.gov/archive/nasa/casi.ntrs.nasa.gov/20080039173.pdf

Howley, Brian *AA236: Overview of Spacecraft Attitude Determination and Control,* Lockheed Martin, avail: https://www.scribd.com/document/95397487/LM-Attitude-Determination-Control.

Johnson, Michael Peter *Mission Control, Inventing the Groundwork of Spaceflight*, U. Press Florida, 2015, ISBN 978-0-8130-6150-4.

Johnson, Michael Peter *Mission Control*, 2015, University Press of Florida, ASIN B01497DZD8.

Kraft, Jr. Christopher C. "Computers and the Space Program: An Overview," Jan. 1976, IBM J. Research & Development.

Kucinskis, Fabrício de Novaes and Ferreira Maurício Gonçalves Vieira *Taking the ECSS Autonomy Concepts One Step Further,* SpaceOps 2010.

Mahmot, Ron; Koslosky, John T.; Beach, Edward; Schwartz, Barbara; *Transportable Payload Operations Control Center Reusable Software: Building Blocks for Quality Ground Data Systems*, N95-17587.

Mandl, Daniel; Koslosky, Jack; Mahmot, Ron; Rackley, Michael; Lauderdale, Jack S*AMPEX Payload Operation Control Center Implementation*, NASA N94-23843.

Marsh, Angela L; Pirani, Joseph L.; Bornas, Nicholas *Operating and Managing a Backup Control Center*, AIAA Paper 201000020234, SpaceOps 2010.

Miau, Jiun-Jih, Holdaway, Richard, *Reducing the Cost of Spacecraft Ground Systems and Operations* (Space Technology Proceedings), 2000, ASIN-B000W2MWOI .

Mudgeway, Douglas J. *Uplink-Downlink: A History of the Deep Space Network, 1957-1997 (The NASA History Series),* Create Space, 2013, ISBN-13: 978-1494740610.

Mudgeway, Douglas J. *Big Dish: Building America's Deep Space Connection to the Planets,* University Press of Florida, 2nd Ed, 2005, ISBN-13: 978-0813028057.

NASA, Space Network User's Guide (SNUG), NASA-450-SNUG.

NASA, Near Earth Network (NEN) User's Guide, Rev. 1, 2010, NASA-453-NENUG.

NASA, esc.gsfc.nasa.gov/space-communications/NEN.html

NASA, *Generic POCC Architecture*, June 30, 1989, NASA-CR-196882.

Rader, Steve; Kearney, Mike; McVittie, Thom; Smith, Dan *Moving Towards a Common Ground and Flight Data Systems Architecture for NASA's Exploration Missions*, NASA/MSFC.

Roddy, Dennis *Satellite Communications*, Fourth Ed, McGraw-Hill Education, 2006, ISBN 0071462988.

Scott, David W. *Using Web 2.0 (and Beyond?) in Space Flight Operations Control Centers*, NASA-MSFC, AIAA paper.

Shirville, Graham; Klofas, Bryan *Genso: A Global Ground Station Network,* avail:*https://www.klofas.com/papers/AMSAT_2007.pdf*

Stakem, Patrick H. *Virtualization and the Cloud*, 2010, 2nd ed, PRRB Publishing, ASIN B00BAFF0JA .

Stakem, Patrick H.; Korol, Guilherme, Gomes; Gabriel August; "A

Lightweight Open Source Command and Control Center and its interface to Cubesats," Proceedings of FSW-15, Flight Software Conference, Johns Hopkins University, Applied Physics Laboratory, October 27-29, 2015. avail: http://flightsoftware.jhuapl.edu/

Stakem, Patrick H.; Martinez, Jose Carlos; Chandrasenan, Vishnu; Mitra, Yash; *A Cubesat Swarm Approach for Exploration of the Asteroid Belt, Presented to NASA Goddard Planetary CubeSats Symposium,* August 16-17, 2018, NASA, GSFC, Greenbelt, MD. (poster presentation)

Tomayko, James E. *Computers in Spaceflight: The NASA Experience,* 1988, NASA Technical Document 19880069935, Amazon digital Services, ASIN B001T4YUI4.

Truszkowski, Walt, *Prototype Software Reuse Environment at Goddard Space Flight Center,* NASA/GSFC, N90-14794.

Wilmot, Jonathan "Use of CCSDS File Delivery Protocol (CFDP) in NASA/GSFC's Flight Software Architecture: core Flight Executive (cFE) and Core Flight System (CFS), NASA/GSFC.

Resources

NASA System Engineering Handbook, NASA/SP-2007-6105 Rev 1.

NASA/GSFC LRO Mission Concept of Operations Summary, Version 1, April 2005.

NASA/GSFC Lunar Reconnaissance Orbiter (LRO) Data Management and Archive Plan, 431-PLAN-000182, Rev. B, May 6, 2013.

NASA, An Overview of the Kalingrad Spaceflight Control Center," TM-87980, May 1986.

"Satellite control, Long-Term Planning and Adoption of Commercial Practices Could Improve DOD's Operations," April 2013, GAO-13-315.

American Institute of Aeronautics and Astronautics, www.aiaa.org

Aviation Week and Space Technology, http://www.aviationweek.com/

Encyclopedia Astronautica, http://www.astronautix.com/

NASA Technical Reports Server, http://ntrs.nasa.gov/

NASA/GSFC Mission Service Evolution Center - https://gmsec.gsfc.nasa.gov/

wikipedia, various..

EOSDIS - *https://earthdata.nasa.gov*

ESA Control Center References

Space Engineering, Spacecraft on-board control procedures, 2008, ECSS-E-ST-70-01C.

Space Engineering, Ground systems and operations – Monitoring and control data definition, 2008, ECSS-E-ST-70-31C.

Space Engineering, Ground Systems and operations, ECSS-E-ST-70C.

Dynamics and Control of Cubesat Orbits for Distributed Space Missions, Aerospace Corporation, http://www.ipam.ucla.edu/wp-content/uploads/2014/10/Aerospace-Corp-project-description-FINAL.pdf

Reference web pages:

CFS - https://cfs.gsfc.nasa.gov/
CFE - http://opensource.gsfc.nasa.gov/projects/cfe/index.php
COSMOS - www.cosmosrb.com
ITOS - http://itos.gsfc.nasa.gov/
www.Space-track.org

Keplerian Elements primer:
http://www.amsat.org/amsat/keps/kepmodel.html

Download the code:

The COSMOS source code:
https://github.com/BallAerospace/COSMOS

The cFS source code:
http://sourceforge.net/projects/coreflightexec/

The CFE source code:
http://sourceforge.net/projects/coreflightexec/

The Integration of cfs and cosmos:
https://github.com/cfspluscosmos/cfs-cosmos

NASA, Ground Data Systems and Mission Operations, State of the
Art of Small Spacecraft Technology. (in update, Sept. 2018)

If you enjoyed this book, you might also be interested in some of these.

Stakem, Patrick H. *16-bit Microprocessors, History and Architecture*, 2013 PRRB Publishing, ISBN-1520210922.

Stakem, Patrick H. *4- and 8-bit Microprocessors, Architecture and History*, 2013, PRRB Publishing, ISBN-152021572X,

Stakem, Patrick H. *Apollo's Computers,* 2014, PRRB Publishing, ISBN-1520215800.

Stakem, Patrick H. *The Architecture and Applications of the ARM Microprocessors,* 2013, PRRB Publishing, ISBN-1520215843.

Stakem, Patrick H. *Earth Rovers: for Exploration and Environmental Monitoring,* 2014, PRRB Publishing, ISBN-152021586X.

Stakem, Patrick H. *Embedded Computer Systems, Volume 1, Introduction and Architecture*, 2013, PRRB Publishing, ISBN-1520215959.

Stakem, Patrick H. *The History of Spacecraft Computers from the V-2 to the Space Station*, 2013, PRRB Publishing, ISBN-1520216181.

Stakem, Patrick H. *Floating Point Computation*, 2013, PRRB Publishing, ISBN-152021619X.

Stakem, Patrick H. *Architecture of Massively Parallel Microprocessor Systems*, 2011, PRRB Publishing, ISBN-1520250061.

Stakem, Patrick H. *Multicore Computer Architecture,* 2014, PRRB Publishing, ISBN-1520241372.

Stakem, Patrick H. *Personal Robots*, 2014, PRRB Publishing, ISBN-1520216254.

Stakem, Patrick H. *RISC Microprocessors, History and Overview,* 2013, PRRB Publishing, ISBN-1520216289.

Stakem, Patrick H. *Robots and Telerobots in Space Applications*, 2011, PRRB Publishing, ISBN-1520210361.

Stakem, Patrick H. *The Saturn Rocket and the Pegasus Missions, 1965,* 2013, PRRB Publishing, ISBN-1520209916.

Stakem, Patrick H. *Visiting the NASA Centers, and Locations of Historic Rockets & Spacecraft,* 2017, PRRB Publishing, ISBN-1549651205.

Stakem, Patrick H. *Microprocessors in Space*, 2011, PRRB Publishing, ISBN-1520216343.

Stakem, Patrick H. Computer *Virtualization and the Cloud*, 2013, PRRB Publishing, ISBN-152021636X.

Stakem, Patrick H. *What's the Worst That Could Happen? Bad Assumptions, Ignorance, Failures and Screw-ups in Engineering Projects, 2014,* PRRB Publishing, ISBN-1520207166.

Stakem, Patrick H. *Computer Architecture & Programming of the Intel x86 Family, 2013,* PRRB Publishing, ISBN-1520263724.

Stakem, Patrick H. *The Hardware and Software Architecture of the Transputer,* 2011,PRRB Publishing, ISBN-152020681X.

Stakem, Patrick H. *Mainframes, Computing on Big Iron*, 2015, PRRB Publishing, ISBN- 1520216459.

Stakem, Patrick H. *Spacecraft Control Centers*, 2015, PRRB Publishing, ISBN-1520200617.

Stakem, Patrick H. *Embedded in Space,* 2015, PRRB Publishing, ISBN-1520215916.

Stakem, Patrick H. *A Practitioner's Guide to RISC Microprocessor Architecture*, Wiley-Interscience, 1996, ISBN-0471130184.

Stakem, Patrick H. *Cubesat Engineering*, PRRB Publishing, 2017, ISBN-1520754019.

Stakem, Patrick H. *Cubesat Operations*, PRRB Publishing, 2017, ISBN-152076717X.

Stakem, Patrick H. *Interplanetary Cubesats*, PRRB Publishing, 2017, ISBN-1520766173 .

Stakem, Patrick H. Cubesat Constellations, Clusters, and Swarms, Stakem, PRRB Publishing, 2017, ISBN-1520767544.

Stakem, Patrick H. *Graphics Processing Units, an overview*, 2017, PRRB Publishing, ISBN-1520879695.

Stakem, Patrick H. *Intel Embedded and the Arduino-101, 2017,* PRRB Publishing, ISBN-1520879296.

Stakem, Patrick H. *Orbital Debris, the problem and the mitigation*, 2018, PRRB Publishing, ISBN-*1980466483*.

Stakem, Patrick H. *Manufacturing in Space*, 2018, PRRB Publishing, ISBN-1977076041.

Stakem, Patrick H. *NASA's Ships and Planes*, 2018, PRRB Publishing, ISBN-1977076823.

Stakem, Patrick H. *Space Tourism*, 2018, PRRB Publishing, ISBN-1977073506.

Stakem, Patrick H. *STEM – Data Storage and Communications*, 2018, PRRB Publishing, ISBN-1977073115.

Stakem, Patrick H. *In-Space Robotic Repair and Servicing*, 2018, PRRB Publishing, ISBN-1980478236.

Stakem, Patrick H. *Introducing Weather in the pre-K to 12 Curricula, A Resource Guide for Educators*, 2017, PRRB Publishing, ISBN-1980638241.

Stakem, Patrick H. *Introducing Astronomy in the pre-K to 12 Curricula, A Resource Guide for Educators*, 2017, PRRB Publishing, ISBN-198104065X.
Also available in a Brazilian Portuguese edition, ISBN-1983106127.

Stakem, Patrick H. *Deep Space Gateways, the Moon and Beyond*, 2017, PRRB Publishing, ISBN-1973465701.

Stakem, Patrick H. *Exploration of the Gas Giants, Space Missions to Jupiter, Saturn, Uranus, and Neptune*, PRRB Publishing, 2018, ISBN-9781717814500.

Stakem, Patrick H. *Crewed Spacecraft*, 2017, PRRB Publishing, ISBN-1549992406.

Stakem, Patrick H. *Rocketplanes to Space*, 2017, PRRB Publishing, ISBN-1549992589.

Stakem, Patrick H. *Crewed Space Stations,* 2017, PRRB Publishing, ISBN-1549992228.

Stakem, Patrick H. *Enviro-bots for STEM: Using Robotics in the pre-K to 12 Curricula, A Resource Guide for Educators,* 2017, PRRB Publishing, ISBN-1549656619.

Stakem, Patrick H. *STEM-Sat, Using Cubesats in the pre-K to 12 Curricula, A Resource Guide for Educators*, 2017, ISBN-1549656376.

Stakem, Patrick H. *Lunar Orbital Platform-Gateway*, 2018, PRRB Publishing, ISBN-1980498628.

Stakem, Patrick H. *Embedded GPU's*, 2018, PRRB Publishing, ISBN- 1980476497.

Stakem, Patrick H. *Mobile Cloud Robotics*, 2018, PRRB Publishing, ISBN- 1980488088.

Stakem, Patrick H. *Extreme Environment Embedded Systems,* 2017, PRRB Publishing, ISBN-1520215967.

Stakem, Patrick H. *What's the Worst, Volume-2*, 2018, ISBN-1981005579.

Stakem, Patrick H., *Spaceports*, 2018, ISBN-1981022287.

Stakem, Patrick H., *Space Launch Vehicles*, 2018, ISBN-1983071773.

Stakem, Patrick H. *Mars*, 2018, ISBN-1983116902.

Stakem, Patrick H. *X-86, 40th Anniversary ed*, 2018, ISBN-1983189405.

Stakem, Patrick H. *Lunar Orbital Platform-Gateway*, 2018, PRRB Publishing, ISBN-1980498628.

Stakem, Patrick H. *Space Weather*, 2018, ISBN-1723904023.

Stakem, Patrick H. *STEM-Engineering Process*, 2017, ISBN-1983196517.

Stakem, Patrick H. *Space Telescopes,* 2018, PRRB Publishing, ISBN-1728728568.

Stakem, Patrick H. *Exoplanets*, 2018, PRRB Publishing, ISBN-9781731385055.

Stakem, Patrick H. *Planetary Defense*, 2018, PRRB Publishing, ISBN-9781731001207.

Patrick H. Stakem *Exploration of the Asteroid Belt*, 2018, PRRB Publishing, ISBN-1731049846.

Patrick H. Stakem *Terraforming*, 2018, PRRB Publishing, ISBN-1790308100.

Patrick H. Stakem, *Martian Railroad,* 2019, PRRB Publishing, ISBN-1794488243.

Patrick H. Stakem, *Exoplanets,* 2019, PRRB Publishing, ISBN-1731385056.

Patrick H. Stakem, *Exploiting the Moon,* 2019, PRRB Publishing, ISBN-1091057850.

Patrick H. Stakem, *RISC-V, an Open Source Solution for Space Flight Computers,* 2019, PRRB Publishing, ISBN-1796434388.

Patrick H. Stakem, *Arm in Space*, 2019, PRRB Publishing, ISBN-9781099789137.

Patrick H. Stakem, *Extraterrestrial Life*, 2019, PRRB Publishing, ISBN-978-1072072188.

Patrick H. Stakem, *Space Command*, 2019, PRRB Publishing, ISBN-978-1693005398.

www.ingramcontent.com/pod-product-compliance
Lightning Source LLC
La Vergne TN
LVHW092342060326
832902LV00008B/767